WASHI
WONDERFUL

An Imprint of Sterling Publishing
387 Park Avenue South
New York, NY 10016

ISBN 978-1-4547-0811-7

Library of Congress Cataloging-in-Publication Data

Doh, Jenny.
Washi wonderful : creative projects & ideas for paper tape / Jenny Doh.
pages cm
Includes bibliographical references and index.
ISBN 978-1-4547-0811-7 (alk. paper)
1. Tape craft. 2. Masking tape. 3. Japanese paper. I. Title.
TT869.7.D64 2014
745.5--dc23

2013028430

LARK CRAFTS and the distinctive Lark logo are registered trademarks of Sterling
Distributed in Canada by Sterling Publishing
c/o Canadian Manda Group, 165 Dufferin Street
Toronto, Ontario, Canada M6K 3H6
Distributed in the United Kingdom by GMC Distribution Services
Castle Place, 166 High Street, Lewes, East Sussex, England BN7 1XU
Distributed in Australia by Capricorn Link (Australia) Pty. Ltd.
P.O. Box 704, Windsor, NSW 2756, Australia

For information about custom editions, special sales, and premium and corporate purchases, please contact Sterling
Special Sales at 800-805-5489 or specialsales@sterlingpublishing.com.

Email academic@larkbooks.com for information about desk and examination copies.
The complete policy can be found at larkcrafts.com.

Manufactured in China

2 4 6 8 10 9 7 5 3 1

larkcrafts.com

WASHI
WONDERFUL

CREATIVE PROJECTS & IDEAS
FOR PAPER TAPE

jenny doh

LARK

CONTENTS

Welcome to Washi Wonderful, where tape is cute and makes any craft project more fun! Washi tape has taken the crafting world by storm since the early 2000s, and it's no secret why. Washi tape is easy to use, it's reusable and repositionable, it comes in just about any color and pattern you can imagine, and it's widely—and inexpensively—available.

But what exactly is washi tape? And what can you do with it? Keep reading for an intimate look at a tape trend that is here to stick.

A STICKY HISTORY

To really understand what washi tape is, we must first look at its history—and more specifically, at the history of washi paper. Washi was first made in Japan more than 1400 years ago. It gets its name from two Japanese words: "wa" meaning "Japanese" and "shi" meaning "paper." Generally, the term "washi" refers to any paper that is traditionally made by hand. Although typically made from fibers of the gampi tree bark, the mitsumata shrub, or paper mulberry, washi can also be made from bamboo, hemp, rice, and wheat. In ancient times, washi was made in the dead of winter, because cold running water was necessary to the long and arduous papermaking process. This age-old paper is sturdy yet slightly transparent, and has been used for centuries in bookbinding, origami, and home décor projects, in addition to all the regular uses of traditional paper.

Fast-forward to the year 2006, when a group of female artists from Tokyo emailed a Japanese masking tape manufacturer, Kamoi Kakoshi®, to express interest in meeting with the company and visiting their masking tape plant. The artists presented them with a book of art they had made using the company's strictly industrial masking tapes, and requested that the company manufacture the masking tape in various colors. Having previously only thought of the tape in purely functional terms, the manufacturing team at Kamoi Kakoshi® was blown away by the innovation of these artists. Development began on colored versions of masking tape, and in 2008, twenty colors of masking tape were presented for sale. The product was dubbed "mt" (short for "masking tape"), and the era of what we affectionately call "washi tape" was born.

BUT WHAT IS WASHI TAPE?

Washi tape is simply masking tape made from rice paper. It has low-tack adhesive on the back, so you can remove it from a surface at any time without damaging the surface in the slightest. It's sold in a roll, and it can be found in a wide array of colors, patterns, and styles. Some washi is more transparent, while some is more opaque. Some washi is ultra glossy and smooth, while some has a grainier textured surface. Washi also comes in a variety of widths, referred to in three ways in this book:

* thin is ³⁄₁₆ to ¼ inch (5 to 6 mm) wide
* standard is ⅝ inch (16 mm) wide
* thick is ¾ to 1¾ inches (19 to 44 mm) wide

Washi tape can be found in a variety of places: online, at your local craft store, even at big retail stores. Its ever-increasing popularity has definitely made finding it that much easier, and has made it less expensive too.

So What Can you Do with Washi Tape?

Perhaps a better question is: What *can't* you do with washi tape? You can stick it on practically anything, including scrapbook pages, cards, kraft paper, cardboard boxes, walls, your refrigerator, plastic containers, and glass jars! Washi tape is both cute and functional. It can secure a photo while enhancing texture, it can hold pieces of paper together while adding color, and it can wrap a gift while increasing style. It's a marvelous way to embellish craft projects and home décor—a quick swipe of washi tape and you have instant interest. The beauty of washi tape is that if you change your mind, you can remove it and reposition it anytime you like.

And What Can you Do To Washi Tape?

You can rip it, cut it, twist it, or sew through it. You can glue small items to it, such as rhinestones, faux flowers, or buttons. And, what's perhaps most fun, you can write on it! Any permanent marker will do the job just fine. Perhaps you want to add words to a photo on a scrapbook page, but you don't want to write directly on the photo—washi tape is the perfect avenue for such a project. Write your desired sentiment on a piece of washi tape and stick the tape over the picture. Should you ever need to remove the photo later, you'll be able to use it or even frame it because you chose not to write directly on it.

You can also stamp on washi tape using any permanent inkpad. With both writing and stamping, you do have to be sure to use permanent inks; with any other type of ink, the surface of washi tape is so smooth that the ink will smear or rub right off. You can also paint on washi tape with acrylic or spray paint. If you want to ensure a permanent adherence of color, you can always spray the painted washi tape with a clear-coat sealer, but paint will usually stay put on its own.

WASHI WONDERFUL

TOOLS AND MATERIALS

Before we dive into the techniques involved with washi tape, let's go over the basic tools and materials you'll need in addition to the tape itself. Start by collecting the tools in the Basic Washi Kit (see sidebar).

In addition, many projects have a paper or cardstock base, and some of the projects will direct you to work with a basic blank greeting card or postcard. These can be purchased at craft stores, often with coordinating envelopes. Or, to make your own greeting card, cut a standard letter-size piece of cardstock in half, then fold one half so it becomes 4¼ x 5½ inches (10.8 x 14 cm); you can then acquire envelopes separately to go with your card. You can also make your own postcard by cutting standard sizes of 4 x 6 inches (10.2 x 15.2 cm) or 5 x 7 inches (12.7 x 17.8 cm) from cardstock. Then you won't need to find an envelope.

Most of the projects will also include some form of ink, usually either a permanent marker or an inkpad. Many projects will include some form of adhesive in addition to washi tape, such as craft glue and double-sided tape. You'll also see mention of glue dots and foam dots in the What You'll Need list of some projects. Glue dots are individual dots that are ultra-adhesive and perfect for adhering a cardstock shape to the front of a card, for example. Foam dots are double-sided sticky pieces of foam that aren't quite as sticky as glue dots, but add space between the surface and the piece you're adhering. If you're looking to add dimension to a project, use foam dots instead of glue dots. Both can be found at your local craft or hobby store.

You'll also notice projects that include kitchen utensils, glass bottles, and wrapped gifts. Because of the wide variety of surfaces washi can be used on, be sure to read through the What You'll Need list at the beginning of each project.

BASIC WASHI KIT

The majority of the projects in this book will use the following materials, so you should have them on hand before you begin:

- Washi: Each project will list the colors and appropriate thicknesses used, for your reference.
- Scissors
- Sharp craft knife
- Self-healing mat
- Metal ruler

WASHI TAPE TECHNIQUE

For the projects in this book, you'll see artists do amazing things with such a seemingly simple material. You will see washi tape twisted and manipulated to spell a lovely sentiment on the front of a card, artistically folded into stunning pieces of jewelry, adhered to transform an ordinary light switch plate, and even used to create a snowman's accessories! Let's first go over a few basic techniques to get you started on the right foot.

Cutting and Ripping

Since washi tape is sold on the roll, the first step in any project will be removing the tape from that roll so you can adhere it to your surface. Similar to masking tape, most washi tape is very easy to rip, so pulling a length of tape and ripping it from the roll is often the easiest way to go. If you want a cleaner edge, however, you can also pull a length of tape and cut it from the roll with a pair of scissors.

Whether you cut or rip, it's best to cut across the width of the washi tape. If you want to cut along its length to make a narrow strip, firmly stick your piece of washi tape on a self-healing cutting mat. Place a metal ruler on top of the tape where you'd like to cut, and press firmly with a sharp craft knife along the edge of the ruler. This will allow you to pull off the thinner pieces of tape without them getting tangled in each other. You can cut a piece of washi in half, thirds, or even narrower using this method. These same tools also work for cutting out small shapes from washi tape, such as triangles, squares, or anything else with straight edges.

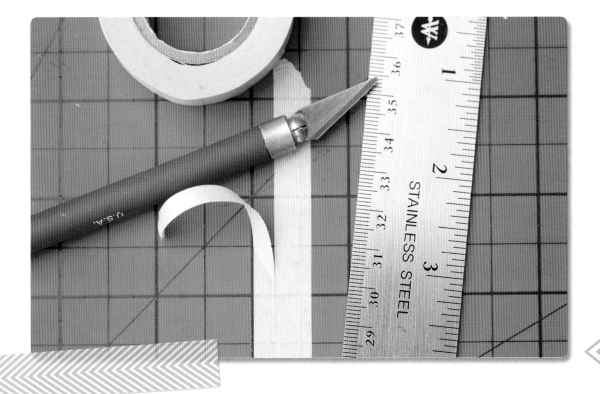

Vellum Method

If you'd like to cut out shapes with rounded edges from washi tape, the easiest way to go about doing this is to use the vellum method. Firmly adhere a piece of washi tape to a piece of translucent vellum paper, then cut out or punch the rounded shape from the washi-covered vellum. Once you have your shape cut, you can peel it off of the vellum and use it in your projects.

You will see vellum used as a stabilizer in this way in many projects throughout this book. In some projects, you will be instructed to stick several pieces of washi onto one piece of translucent vellum, slightly overlapping the tape pieces next to each other to completely cover the vellum. This will allow you to cut or punch out larger shapes before peeling off the cut shape and using it.

You'll see other projects in this book that use this method, but they don't instruct you to peel the shape off of the vellum. In these projects, vellum is used as a stabilizer so you can glue a washi-covered piece onto your project. Whether you need to peel the washi off the vellum or not will always be noted in the project instructions.

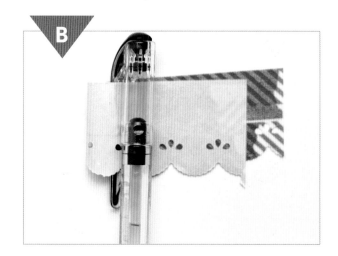

If the project instructions do include peeling the washi shape off of the vellum, you will notice quickly that peeling can be quite tricky, especially when working with small or complicated shapes. For larger pieces, put a portion of the shape through a pen cap with a clip, then rotate the pen cap so that the washi shape peels onto the pen cap (figs. A, B, and C). For tiny shapes, stick the edge of your sharp craft knife or the end of a push pin in between the vellum and washi to peel it (figs. D and E).

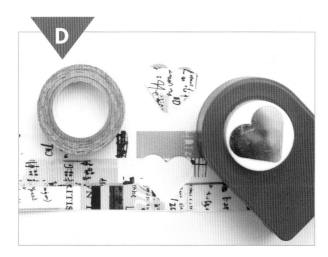

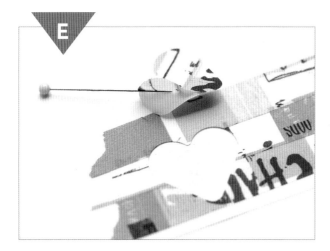

Transparency Method

In addition to vellum, some of the projects in this book use transparency sheets as a stabilizer for washi. Similar to the vellum method, you can stick pieces of washi tape onto a transparency sheet (fig. A). Then you can turn it over, draw words or shapes (fig. B), and cut them out with scissors (fig. C). Peel off the shapes as you would with the vellum method (p. 12) and stick it onto your project (fig. D).

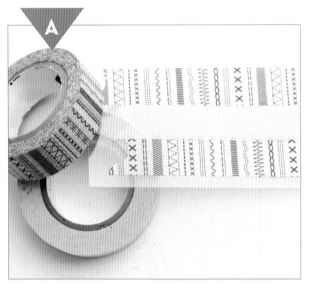

A

B

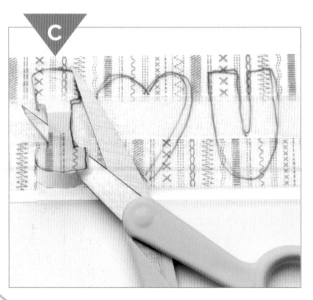

C

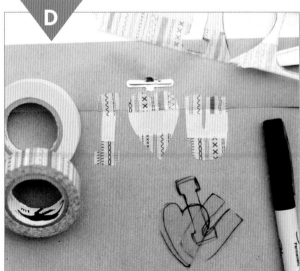

D

WASHI WONDERFUL

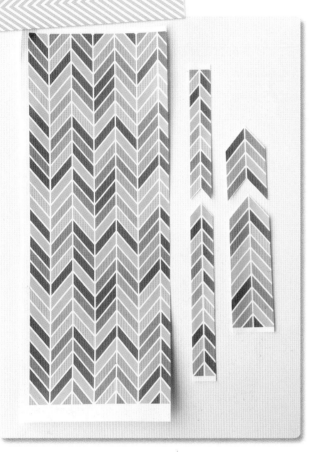

A FINAL NOTE

In the rest of the projects in this book, you will see that the word "washi" is used rather than the full "washi tape." So, note that whenever you see the word "washi," we are referring to "washi tape."

MAKING YOUR OWN WASHI TAPE

Even though there are countless washi tape options available to you, you may find on occasion that you want to make your own. If so, the simplest method is to start with plain white masking tape and then add patterns, doodles, or words in permanent marker, ink, or paint.

On page 123, the designer teaches another way to make your own washi tape using printer paper and rubber cement. In this case, dried rubber cement acts as the low-tack adhesive in place of the sticky washi tape back.

CREATIVE STORAGE SOLUTIONS

Washi tape is fun to use in craft projects. It's also fun to find ways to creatively store and display the colorful rolls! Shown here are just a few examples of how you can organize your stash of washi tape—ideas that can fit almost any crafting space:

- A vintage seed packet display (fig. A) is a fantastic place to store washi tape because of its many small compartments. Keep your eye open for wooden drawers and displays with small compartments as you visit local thrift stores and antique shops, and you just may find something similarly useful and attractive.

- Wooden embroidery hoops come in assorted sizes and can hold many rolls of washi tape. Use just the outer ring that can be opened up to insert the washi tape rolls onto the hoop and then secure the hoop closed with the metal screw (fig. B). Keep the hoop on your desk or hang it on a wall or bulletin board.

- If you have an old frame without the glass or backing, you can create a display unit by stapling a piece of chicken wire to the back side of the frame. Once that's done, twist paper clips to become hooks that can hang washi tape rolls onto the chicken wire (fig. C).

- Vintage sewing boxes have lots of little compartments and drawers that can be used to store washi tape rolls (fig. D). Keep the lids and drawers open to show off your washi rolls or keep them closed and out of sight when not in use.

- The next time you're done using your roll of aluminum foil, don't throw the carton out! Simply take out the cardboard roll, place the washi tape onto the roll and place it back into the foil container. When you are ready to use the washi, peel off a length that you need and use the serrated blade on the container to neatly cut it off (fig. E).

- A wire pants hanger is designed with wire at the top and then a sturdy thin paper tube at the bottom. Unsnap that tube from the wire and insert the washi tape onto the tube and then snap it back onto the wire (fig. F).

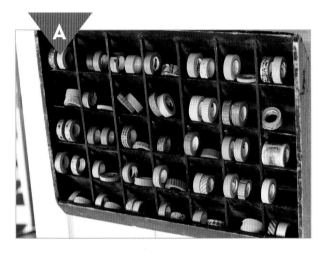

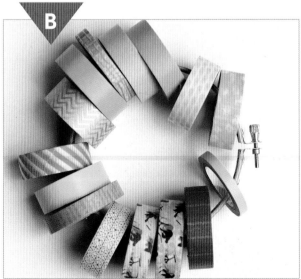

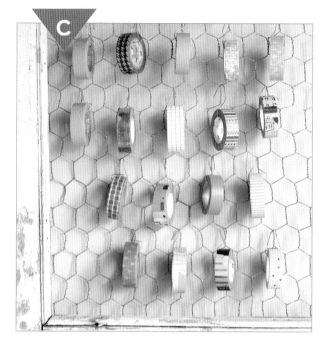

A handmade card with heartfelt sentiments is really the ultimate gift for most people. This chapter shows you how to make inventive cards with washi for almost every occasion!

thank you CARDS

Don't have alphabet stamps on hand? Don't love your handwriting? No problem! With a bit of clever maneuvering, washi can become the only letters you'll ever need.

DESIGNER: Avital

WHAT YOU'LL NEED

Basic Washi Kit, page 9
Washi:
- Dotted yellow, standard
- Striped black, thick
- Dotted red, standard

2 blank cards:
- White, 5½ x 4¼ inches (14 x 10.8 cm)
- Kraft-colored, 4¼ x 5½ inches (10.8 x 14 cm)

Bamboo skewer

Sewing machine
3 small buttons
Hand-sewing needle and thread
Alphabet stickers
Alphabet stamps (optional)
1 sheet of translucent vellum
Heart-shaped paper punches:
- 1 inch (2.5 cm)
- ½ inch (1.3 cm)

WHAT YOU DO

Thanks a Bunch Card

1 Stick a long strip of dotted yellow washi onto the self-healing cutting mat. With the ruler and sharp craft knife, cut the strip into thirds or even fourths horizontally. This will give you strips of washi measuring ⅛–³⁄₁₆ inch (3–5 mm) wide.

2 Carefully remove one of the thin strips and start placing it down onto the front of the card to form script-style letters for the word "thanks." Don't worry about sizing it perfectly. Manipulate the tape as needed using your fingers and the

bamboo skewer, especially in tricky curves and loops.

3 Using the ruler as a guide, align the letters at the bottom and the top by making cuts with the sharp craft knife. Use very light strokes with the sharp craft knife so only the washi gets cut and not the card underneath. Remember that washi is very thin, so you don't need a lot of strength to cut through it.

4 Stitch a straight horizontal line at the top of all the letters with a

sewing machine. Stitch a second line at the bottom of all the letters. It's okay for some of the stitches to catch some of the washi edges.

5 Using the needle and thread, make X stitches on three small buttons, then knot to secure the thread. Attach these buttons to the card with glue dots. Add small alphabet stickers to spell "a bunch." If you don't have alphabet stickers, you can use alphabet stamps.

THX Card

1 Stick a piece of striped black washi onto translucent vellum. Punch out one small heart and two tiny hearts (see Vellum Method, page 12).

2 Carefully peel the small washi heart from the vellum and stick it onto the front of the kraft-colored card in the position shown. Save the tiny punched hearts for step 7.

3 Stick a long strip of dotted red washi onto the self-healing cutting mat. Cut the strip in half horizontally with the ruler and the sharp craft knife. This will give you thin strips of washi approximately ¼ inch (6 mm) wide.

4 Carefully remove one of the strips of washi from the cutting mat, then cut several smaller pieces that are approximately 1½ to 2 inches (3.8 to 5.1 cm) long. Use these smaller pieces to form the letters THX and stick them to the front of the card.

5 Using the ruler as a guide, align the letters at the bottom and the top by making cuts with the sharp craft knife. Use very light strokes with the sharp craft knife so that only

the washi gets cut and not the card underneath.

6 Repeat step 3, but use the striped black washi and cut the strips even thinner, so they are approximately ⅛ inch (3 mm) wide. Repeat steps 4 and 5 with these thinner strips to form the two tiny X's beneath the THX, leaving room for the hearts.

7 Carefully peel the tiny punched hearts from the taped vellum pieces in step 2 and stick them in between the two tiny X's.

8 Sew a line of zigzag stitching at the top edge of the THX with a sewing machine.

diagonal window THANK YOU CARD

Designer: Avital

Creative Idea: Use a ruler and a pencil to draw two diagonal lines across the front of the card. Cut along both lines. Set aside the top portion (still attached to the back of the card) and the bottom cut portion. Trace the middle cutout portion onto translucent vellum with a pencil and cover it with washi. Cut the vellum along the traced lines and reassemble the card front, taping the vellum in place on the back side.

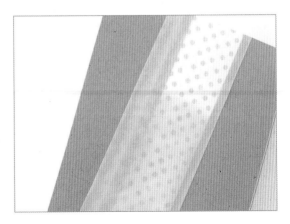

WASHI WONDERFUL

circle window
THANK YOU CARD

Designer: Avital

Creative Idea: Punch a hole in the front of a card with a large circle paper punch. Stick strips of washi onto translucent vellum and punch it out with a slightly larger circle paper punch. Adhere it to the inside of the punched card.

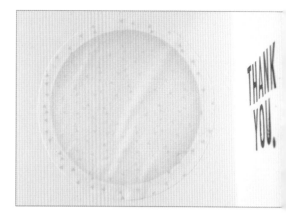

hearts and scallop-edge CARD

Designer: Avital

Creative Idea: Open
a blank white card and stick a
standard piece of washi to the
inside right edge of the card.
Punch those two corners of the
card with a rounded corner punch.
Punch the front right edge of card
with a scallop-edge punch.

collaged and cut
I LOVE YOU CARDS

One piece of washi-covered vellum provides all of the embellishments for these darling cards from the heart. Simply punch out various shapes and letters to spell out your desired sentiment.

DESIGNER: Avital

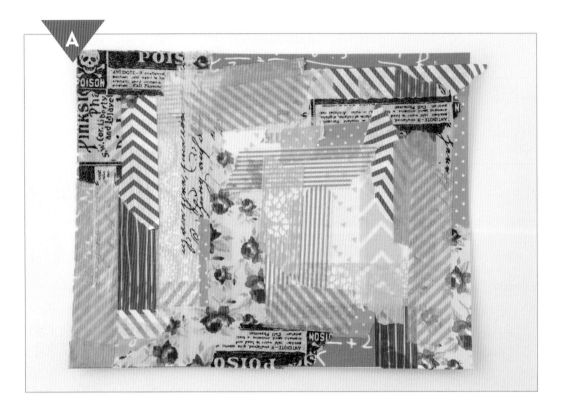

WHAT YOU'LL NEED

Basic Washi Kit, page 9
Washi: assorted colors and patterns, standard
1 blank top-folding cream-colored card,
    4¼ x 5½ inches (10.8 x 14 cm)
1 blank side-folding cream-colored card,
    4¼ x 5½ inches (10.8 x 14 cm)
1 sheet of translucent vellum
Gel medium
Small paintbrush
Rounded corner paper punch
Letter-shaped paper punches
Heart-shaped paper punches, various sizes
Clear liquid adhesive
1 piece of ½-inch (1.3 cm) wide pink ribbon,
    12 inches (30.5 cm) long
Foam dots

WHAT YOU DO

1 To create a washi collage, tear pieces of washi in varying colors, widths, and lengths and stick them onto a piece of translucent vellum (see Vellum Method, page 12). Work from the edges of the vellum in toward the center, allowing the strips to overlap from side to side and from top to bottom until you eventually fill the entire area. Apply a layer of gel medium to the taped vellum piece with a small paintbrush and let it dry (fig. A).

2 Punch letters and hearts out of the taped vellum piece with the paper punches.

3 Round the lower corners of the top-folding card and the upper and lower right corners of the side-folding card with the rounded corner paper punch.

4 Adhere one punched heart and punched letters that spell "I" and "YOU" onto the upper portion of the top-folding card with clear liquid adhesive. Tie a bow with the pink ribbon around the center of the card.

5 Adhere punched letters and smaller punched hearts onto the side-folding card with clear liquid adhesive. Attach the larger hearts to the card with foam dots.

WASHI WONDERFUL

welcome little one
CARD

DESIGNER: Avital

WHAT YOU'LL NEED

Basic Washi Kit, page 9
Washi:
- Patterned multicolored, standard
- Yellow striped, standard

1 blank white card, 4¼ x 5½ inches (10.8 x 14 cm)
Rounded corner paper punch
Glitter tape, ⅜-inch (9.5 mm) wide
Glitter alphabet stickers
Sewing machine

A quick folding technique turns one long piece of washi into a pretty pleat for this sweet and touching card, sure to put a smile on the face of new parents.

WHAT YOU DO

1 Punch the lower corners of the card, front and back, with the rounded corner punch.

2 To make the pleats:
- Stick the end of a roll of patterned multicolored washi horizontally on the lower left section of the card, without cutting the tape from the roll.
- Start pleating the washi by sticking down a small section, and then backing up to overlap the tape, fold it, stick it on itself, and go forward again.
- Repeat this process until you reach the right-hand edge. Cut the washi so it is even with the edge of the card. You can make the pleats look neat with precise intervals or messy with imprecise intervals. You can always carefully lift the washi and redo the pleats as you go.

3 Stick additional strips of striped yellow washi above the pleated strip of washi, allowing them to slightly overlap one another. Trim.

4 Center a strip of glitter tape over the section where the pleated washi and non-pleated washi meet, to cover the seam.

5 Add a zigzag stitch along the entire length of the glitter tape with the sewing machine.

6 Stick glitter alphabet stickers to the washi to create your sentiment.

twisted flower CARD

Twist, crinkle, and bend one continuous length of washi for this fun and funky flower card that's perfect for any occasion.

DESIGNER: Avital

WHAT YOU'LL NEED

Basic Washi Kit, page 9
Washi:
- Green, standard
- Striped multi-colored, standard

1 blank white card, 4¼ x 5½ inches (10.8 x 14 cm)
2 colored pencils in different shades of green
Baby powder
Tiny foam dots
1 small red button
Hand-sewing needle and thread
Glue dot
Alphabet stickers

WHAT YOU DO

1 Make a border by drawing straight lines with a green colored pencil and the ruler on all four sides of the card. Draw a second set of connected straight lines slightly smaller than the first set, with a different shade of green.

2 Stick the end of the striped multi-colored washi (without cutting it from its roll) to the center of the card. This will be the center of the flower (fig. A).

3 Twist, squish, and roll the washi around the center of the flower to create a crinkly texture. Continue in this manner until you reach your desired flower size, then cut the washi from its roll and tuck the end under one of the twisted sections (fig. B).

4 Eliminate stickiness by sprinkling baby powder on the exposed sticky parts of the tape. Shake off the excess.

5 Cut a tiny leaf from green washi. Place a tiny foam dot on the center back of the leaf and stick it onto the card, tucked beneath the flower. Repeat with as many additional leaves as desired.

6 Stitch an X on the red button with the needle and thread, then tie and secure. Adhere the button to the center of the flower with the glue dot.

7 Press alphabet stickers below the flower to spell out a message.

A

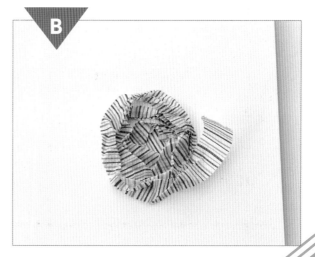

B

welcome to the neighborhood
CARDS

Every inch of these charming cards is filled with tiny details that are made up of—you guessed it—washi! From the houses and chimneys to the trees and bunting, colorful washi is used to the fullest in this colorful project.

DESIGNER:
Ishtar Olivera Belart

WHAT YOU'LL NEED

Basic Washi Kit, page 9
Washi: assorted coordinating patterns and colors
2 blank kraft-colored cards and matching envelopes:
- 8¼ x 4 inches (21 x 10.2 cm)
- 7 x 5 inches (17.8 x 12.7 cm)
Gel pens: white, pink, green, blue

WHAT YOU DO

Houses in a Row Card

1 Cut a piece of thick washi into the shape of a rectangle and stick it onto the bottom edge of an oblong card for the lower part of the house. Cut a coordinating piece of washi tape into the shape of a trapezoid and stick it above the first piece of washi to make the roof. For a taller house, add a second piece of washi to the bottom part of the house before adding the roof piece.

2 Repeat step 1 with assorted washi to make a row of houses along the bottom edge of the card. Cut some of the roofs into triangles instead of trapezoids.

3 Cut out tiny pieces of washi and stick them onto the houses for windows, doors, and chimneys.

4 Doodle flowers, trees, and lines for banners using gel pens.

5 Cut out ovals to make a tree and tiny triangles to create a banner.

6 Use similar methods to decorate the coordinating envelope. If you want to mail the card, be sure to leave room on the envelope for the postage and address.

WHAT YOU DO

Houses in a Field Card

1 Cut a piece of washi into the shape of a rectangle and stick it onto any section of the card. Draw a trapezoid-shaped roof above the washi with a white gel pen and fill it in. Cut tiny pieces of washi in different colors and stick them onto the house to make a window and chimney.

2 Cut a piece of washi into an oval and stick it anywhere on the card. Add lines with a white gel pen to make that shape become a tree. Add more small doodles with a gel pen (fig. A).

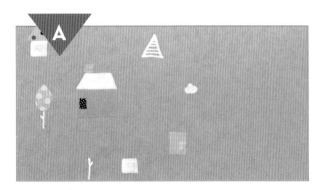

3 Repeat steps 1 and 2 in different areas of the card until the entire card is filled with houses, trees, and tiny doodles (fig. B).

bow for baby CARD

Designer: Avital

Creative Idea: To make a washi bow, cut a 6-inch (15.2 cm) strip of washi. Connect the ends to make a washi ring, with the sticky part on the inside of the ring. Sprinkle baby powder inside the ring to remove the stickiness. Shake off the excess. Wrap the bow center with a narrow strip of washi, glue it to a card, and decorate it with threaded button.

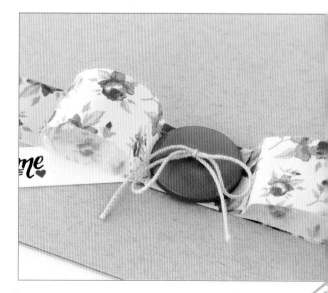

birthday CARDS

Add personality and whimsy to the next birthday card you make with clever uses of washi. In these quirky cards, washi and vellum combine to create not only fun shapes but also friendly sentiments.

DESIGNER: Ishtar Olivera Belart

WHAT YOU'LL NEED

Basic Washi Kit, page 9
Washi:

- Hot pink: thin
- Brown: standard
- Patterned tan: standard
- Red: standard
- Other assorted patterns and colors as desired

2 blank kraft-colored cards, each 5 Inches (12.7 cm) square

1 sheet of translucent vellum paper

Glue stick

White cardstock scrap

Scallop-edged paper punch

WHAT YOU DO

Slice of Cake Card

1 Cut a scrap of white cardstock into two strips measuring 3 x ½ inches (7.6 x 1.3 cm). Place the pieces onto your workspace side by side so the long edges are touching each other. Connect the two pieces with a thin piece of hot pink washi. Slightly trim one of the short sides so that there is a slight curve. This will be the bottom portion of the cake slice. Cut tiny pieces of brown washi and attach them to the cake slice for sprinkles.

2 Sketch a triangle for the cake frosting onto a piece of vellum. Attach strips of patterned tan washi to the vellum, and then cut out the shape (see Vellum Method, page 12). Repeat this process to make a red circle for the fruit garnish.

3 Use the glue stick to adhere the bottom portion of the cake onto the front of a square card. Peel the cake frosting from the vellum backing and attach it to the top of the cake slice. Peel the fruit garnish from the vellum backing and attach it to the cake slice.

4 Continue using the Vellum Method to make candles, scallop bunting, and a punched scalloped edge. Adhere them to the card.

Sunburst Card

1 Use the Vellum Method to make a circle with a 1¼-inch (3.2 cm) diameter, as well as several thin strips in assorted colors and patterns. These strips should vary in length, approximately ½ to 2 inches (1.3 to 5.1 cm).

2 Peel the strips from the vellum and attach them onto a square card to make a circular shape. Peel the circle from the vellum and attach it in the center of the strips.

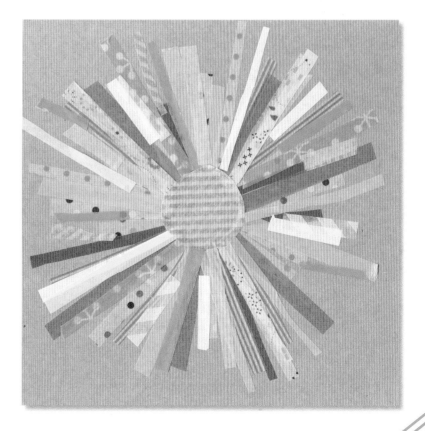

WASHI WONDERFUL

winter holiday CARDS

DESIGNER:

Ishtar Olivera Belart

WHAT YOU'LL NEED

Basic Washi Kit, page 9
Washi:
- White, standard
- Gold, standard
- Dotted gold, standard
- Striped gold, thick
- Red, standard
- Other assorted patterns and colors as desired

2 blank cards:
- 5 x 4 inches (12.7 x 10.2 cm)
- 5 inches (12.7 cm) square

1 sheet of translucent vellum
Bird-shaped paper punch
Flower-shaped paper punch
White acrylic paint
Small paintbrush
White gel pen

A fancy punched bird tops a washi tree to welcome winter, and on the next page, amiable painted snowmen are decked out in their finest washi accessories.

WHAT YOU DO

Dove Card

1 Cut a strip of white washi that's approximately 4½ inches (11.4 cm) long. Trim both long sides of the washi so it feels slightly wonky and uneven. Stick this onto the center of the rectangular card lengthwise to make the tree trunk.

2 Cut and trim additional strips of white washi and stick them onto the first piece to make branches.

3 Cut small leaf shapes out of solid, dotted, and striped gold washi and stick them onto the branches and near the bottom of the tree trunk.

4 Stick strips of striped gold washi onto vellum paper so that they slightly overlap. Punch out the shape of a bird. Punch a small flower shape on the lower portion of the bird (fig. A).

5 Peel off the vellum backing and stick the bird above the tree trunk.

Snowmen Card

1 To make a snowman, paint two circles—one above the other—on the square card. Paint a second, smaller snowman next to the first.

2 Make snow on the ground by drawing tiny dots with the white gel pen. Draw slightly larger dots on the upper section of the card to make falling snow.

3 Cut a triangle-shaped hat from striped gold washi and stick it onto the first snowman. Cut a smaller triangle from red washi and stick it onto the second snowman (fig. B).

4 Cut tiny strips of washi in assorted colors to make arms, hat pompoms, and scarves. Draw a tiny bird with the white gel pen, and add a miniature hat and pompom made from red washi.

i love you to pieces COLLAGE CARDS

Designer: Avital

Creative Idea: Apply strips of washi directly to a card surface or to a sheet of vellum (see page 12) that you cut out and adhere to a card. Play with other materials and techniques—such as cardstock and tulle cutouts, stamping and embossing, and alphabet stickers—to add your own creative touches.

bridal shower
INVITATIONS

DIY invitations are taken to a new level with washi and a sewing machine. Use the same patterned washi throughout the invitation suite for a cohesive look. Repeat the instructions to make as many invitations as you need for your event.

WHAT YOU DO

1 Punch the right edge of the blank card front with the scallop-edged paper punch. Punch the lower right corner of the card front with a circle paper punch (fig. A).

2 Prepare the text for the inside of the invitation on your computer, making sure that the text is centered and fits comfortably within a 4¾ x 6½-inch (12 x 16.5 cm) space. Print this text onto the piece of vellum.

3 Cut the printed vellum to measure 4¾ x 6½ inches (12 x 16.5 cm). Save the trimmed vellum scraps.

4 Adhere the printed and trimmed vellum to the inside right of the folded card, using very small pieces of double-sided tape.

5 Stick a 7-inch (17.8 cm) piece of washi on the edge of one of the scraps of vellum from step 3. Punch the edge with the scallop-edged paper punch.

DESIGNER:
Cynthia Shaffer

WHAT YOU'LL NEED

Basic Washi Kit, page 9
Washi: patterned peach/
    cream/tan, standard
Computer and inkjet printer
1 sheet of translucent vellum
    (per invitation)
1 blank cream-colored card
    and matching envelope,
    5 x 7 inches (12.7 x 17.8 cm)
    (per invitation)
Double-sided tape
Scallop-edged paper punch
Circle paper punch, 1-inch
    (2.5 cm)
Sewing machine
Brown and white thread

Please join us for a
bridal shower
honoring

Kaitlynn Patterson

Sunday October 20th
At 2:00 pm

The Patterson Residence

Hosted by Abby

RSVP by October 6th

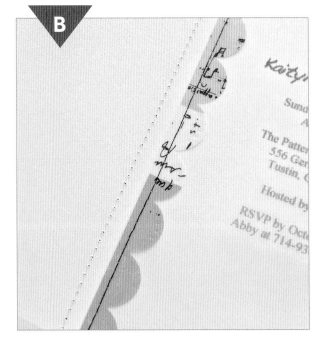

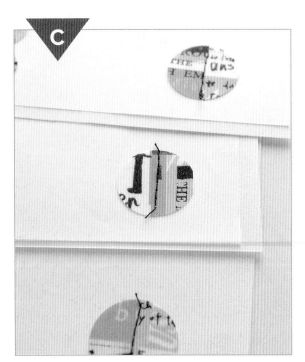

6 Peel the washi off the vellum and stick it onto the vellum panel, aligning the straight edge of the washi with the left long edge of the vellum. Allow the short edges to extend beyond the vellum slightly. Trim the excess washi with scissors (fig. B).

7 Stick small strips of washi onto another scrap of vellum, allowing the strips to slightly overlap. Punch a circle out of this washi-covered piece. Peel the washi off the vellum and stick it toward the lower right of the vellum panel, aligned with the punched hole on the card front (fig. C).

8 Stick a 7-inch (17.8 cm) piece of washi onto the cutting mat. Cut it in half lengthwise using the ruler and the sharp craft knife. Stick one of the halves close to

the fold of the front of the card, allowing the short ends to extend beyond the card slightly. Trim excess with scissors.

9 Add straight stitches to the washi circle, scallop strip, and thin strip with a sewing machine. Allow the stitches to go through the washi and the paper layers (fig. D).

10 For the coordinating envelope, stick a length of washi on the lower portion of the flap. Make scallops with a scallop-edged paper punch. Add straight stitches with a sewing machine. Trim excess thread with scissors.

11 Repeat steps 1 through 10 to make as many invitations as you need for your event.

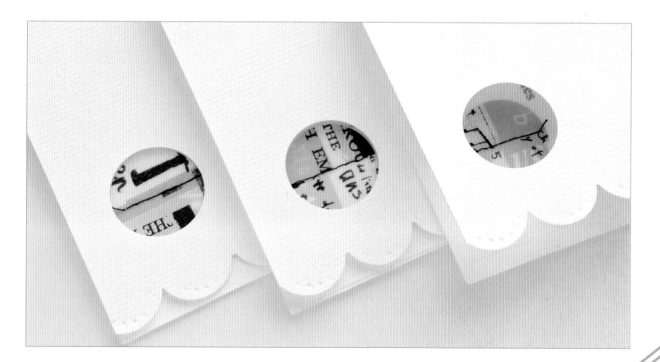

Use washi to make flowers, tassels, sassy stick dolls, and more—to embellish and elevate the gifts that you wrap and give.

seashells GIFT WRAP

Designer: Jenny Doh

Creative Idea #1: Cut a strip of washi and place a bamboo skewer onto the sticky side of the washi lengthwise. Wrap and roll the washi around the entire length of the skewer and cut it into two pieces. Adhere a shell on one end with a glue dot.

Creative Idea #2: To make a washi wave, stick a strip of thick washi onto a piece of vellum. Turn the vellum over and freehand draw a waves pattern and cut it out. Peel the cutout and stick it onto the gift.

sassy stick DOLLS

Transform wooden craft sticks into cheerful gift box toppers by using colorful washi for clothing and a dash of paint for faces. These happy dolls are sure to make any recipient smile.

DESIGNER: Ishtar Olivera Belart

WHAT YOU'LL NEED

Basic Washi Kit, page 9
Washi:
- Patterned navy, thick
- Hot pink, thick
- White, standard

Wooden craft sticks:
  ¾ x 3¾ inches
  (1.9 x 9.5 cm)

White and black acrylic
  paint
Small paintbrush
Container with water
Black fine-point marker
Fluorescent pink gel pen
1 sheet of translucent vellum
Small gift package
Baker's twine

WHAT YOU DO

1 Toward one end of the wooden craft stick, paint a small circle for the face with white acrylic paint and the small paintbrush. Let the paint dry and rinse the paintbrush.

2 Paint the hair around the face area with black acrylic paint. Let the paint dry and rinse the paintbrush.

3 Draw facial features with the black fine-point marker.

4 Draw cheeks with the fluorescent pink gel pen.

5 "Dress" the doll by covering the rest of the stick with pieces of washi.

6 Attach the doll to a gift package with baker's twine.

VARIATIONS FOR DRESSING THE DOLLS

* Use the Vellum Method (page 12) to make a ruffled skirt approximately 1½ inches (3.8 cm) wide. Fold small pleats in the taped vellum piece and attach it to the stick with another piece of washi.
* Use the Vellum Method to cut ears, feathers, hats, ponchos, and other accessories or features to attach to the sticks.
* Make designs on top of the washi with a white gel pen.
* Paint the hair in a variety of styles to create different types of characters. On some dolls, leave out the hair completely.

WASHI WONDERFUL

bows, tags, and
GIFT BAGS

Designer: Ishtar Olivera Belart

Creative Idea #1: To make washi bows, adhere strips of washi to a 4-inch (10.2 cm) square of translucent vellum, evenly spacing out the strips and switching between colors to create a pattern. Fan-fold the taped vellum so there are approximately five ridges. Pinch the folded paper at the center and secure it by wrapping a piece of washi around the center several times.

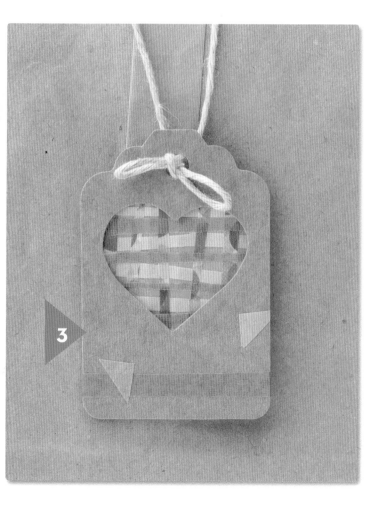

Creative Idea #2: For a scalloped edge, adhere a piece of washi horizontally along the top edge of the bag. Punch all the way across washi-covered edge with a scallop-edged punch.

Creative Idea #3: To make a washi heart tag, stick assorted pieces of washi onto a piece of translucent vellum. Punch a tag out of kraft-colored cardstock, then punch a heart at the top of the tag. Center the washi vellum behind the heart shape and adhere.

small gift BOXES

Designer: Ishtar Olivera Belart

Creative Idea #1: To make the box, trace box Template A (page 140) onto cardstock and cut it out. Use a sharp craft knife to make slits in marked spots, stick small pieces of washi onto the cutout and assemble the box.

Creative Idea #2: To make the bow, cover a 7 x 3-inch (17.8 x 7.6 cm) piece of translucent vellum with strips of washi. Turn the vellum over and trace bow Templates B and C (page 141) onto the vellum. Cut them out. Without peeling off the vellum, fold the left and right sides of the longer bow toward the center and attach with washi. Center the bow button beneath the folded bow and secure in the center with a narrow strip of washi.

WASHI WONDERFUL

patched and pieced GIFT WRAP

Designer: Ishtar Olivera Belart

Creative Idea: Cut and/or tear assorted papers into irregular shapes in varying sizes. Arrange the pieces on your workspace, allowing some to overlap. Attach all of the pieces together with washi. Once the gift wrap is the approximate size that you want, trim the edges with scissors and use it to wrap your gift!

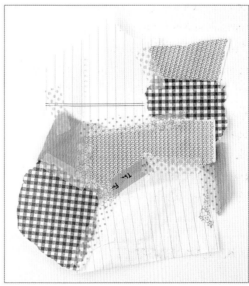

boxed GIFTS

Designer: Carolyn Garris

Creative Idea: To cover the lid of a 4-inch gift box, cut a strip of washi to measure 6 inches (15.2 cm) long and stick it onto the edge of the lid, allowing the ends to fold down over the sides and up inside the lid. Apply more strips, each one abutting the previous strip until the entire lid is covered with washi. To finish, cover the sides of the lid with one long continuous strip of washi.

upcycled GIFT BAGS

Designer: Avital

Creative Idea #1: For the doily bag, fold a doily in half. Stick pieces of washi on the inner half-circle of the doily, allowing them to slightly overlap one another. Lightly sketch the curve of the doily's inner circle directly on the washi with a pencil. Carefully remove the washi in one piece and cut along the traced line. Stick the circle back on the doily. Place the doily onto the folded bag and zigzag-stitch through all thicknesses.

Creative Idea #2: For the washi tag, freehand trim a piece of cardstock into an oval shape. Stick small pieces of washi to the top of the oval. Zigzag stitch along the center of the tag. Punch a hole at the top of the tag and attach it to the bag with a piece of string.

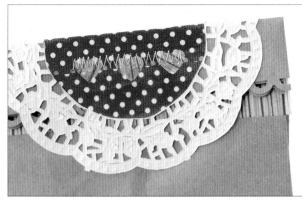

WASHI WONDERFUL

washi winterland GIFTS

DESIGNER: Carolyn Garris

WHAT YOU'LL NEED

Basic Washi Kit, page 9
Washi:
- Dotted black, standard
- Patterned black, standard
- Striped blue/white, standard
- Patterned blue/orange, standard
- Dotted red, standard
- Orange, standard
- Patterned red, standard

Less than 1 skein of white worsted
   weight acrylic yarn*
1 piece of cardboard, 2 x 4 inches
   (5.1 x 10.2 cm)
Black cardstock
Tacky craft glue
Clear liquid adhesive
Hole punches, one ⅛-inch (3 mm)
   and one ¼ inch (6 mm)
Kraft paper
Rubber stamps
Inkpads: gray, white, and black
Small brown paper bag
Alphabet stamps
Metal container with lid
Strong-bonding glue

*I used the Super Savor Red Heart
   worsted weight yarn, which has 364
   yards. That's a lot of pom-poms! You
   can buy smaller skeins offered by
   different manufacturers.*

Pom-pom snowmen are the stars of the show in this project, but they couldn't do what they do without festive washi. Use washi not only to wrap the gifts, but also for the snowmen's scarves, eyes, noses, and top hats!

WHAT YOU DO

Pom-pom Snowman Construction

1 Wrap the yarn horizontally around the piece of cardboard, approximately 50 times (fig. A on page 59).

2 Cut a piece of yarn approximately 5 inches (12.7 cm) long. Carefully remove the wrapped yarn from the cardboard and place it on top of the piece of yarn as shown. Tie the wrapped yarn very tightly and make a double knot (fig. B).

3 Cut the loops open with scissors and trim the yarn to make it into a pompom (fig. C).

4 Repeat steps 1 through 3 to make a second pom-pom for the upper body of the snowman. Trim the second pom-pom shorter to make it slightly smaller than the first pom-pom, but on this second pom-pom, don't trim the piece of yarn used to secure the wrapped yarn. We'll use it in a later step (fig. D).

5 Glue the smaller pom-pom to the slightly larger pom-pom using tacky craft glue.

Snowman Accessories

The Hat

1 Cut black cardstock pieces as follows:

* Circle, 1 inch (2.5 cm) in diameter
* Rectangle, ¾ x 2½ inches (1.9 x 6.4 cm)

2 Place the rectangle piece on your work surface horizontally. Stick a piece of patterned black washi onto the piece. Cut and stick a thin strip of dotted or patterned red washi onto the lower bottom edge (fig. E).

3 Make a ring with the washi rectangle by pulling one short side slightly over the opposite short side, allowing an overlap of about ¼ inch (6 mm). Glue the overlap with the clear liquid adhesive. Let it dry (fig. F).

4 Punch a hole with the ⅛-inch (3 mm) hole punch at the center of the circle piece of cardstock from step 1.

5 Center and glue the bottom edge of the ring from step 3 to the circle piece. Let it dry (fig. G).

6 Pull the string attached to the smaller pom-pom through the hole in the hat and then glue that hat onto the snowman's head with the strong-bonding glue. If you do not want to hang the snowman on your gift, just trim the yarn rather than threading it through the hat.

The Nose

1 To make the nose, roll a tiny piece of orange washi several times to make a skinny carrot (fig. H).

2 Dip one end of the carrot into clear liquid adhesive and then poke that end into the face of the snowman.

The Scarf

1 Cut a piece of striped blue/white washi to measure 7 inches (17.8 cm) long. Fold it in half horizontally so it sticks to itself with the long sides aligned.

2 Cut fringe or an inverted V on the ends (fig. I).

3 Wrap the washi around the snowman's neck and glue it at the point of intersection with clear liquid adhesive.

Buttons and Eyes

1 To make the buttons, stick a piece of dotted black washi onto black cardstock. Punch ¼-inch (6 mm) holes to make circles. Glue the punched holes onto the body of the snowman.

2 For the eyes, cut smaller circles from the black cardstock and glue them to the snowman's face with clear liquid adhesive.

Adorned Packages

Use the washi snowman to adorn assorted gift packages:

* Stamp a piece of kraft paper with holiday-themed rubber stamps, using the gray, white, and black inkpads. Wrap a gift with the paper and stick a piece of washi onto the hanging string to adhere the snowman.
* Stamp a brown paper bag with alphabet stamps, fold over the top edge, and seal it shut with a piece of washi. Stick a piece of washi onto the hanging string to adhere the snowman.
* Stick a piece of washi along the circumference of the lid from a metal container. Glue a snowman to the top of the lid with stronghold glue.

pinwheel gift ensemble
FOR BABY

Decorated gift wrap and a simple garland for a baby shower are made all the more special with the addition of pinwheels. There's something so innocent and sweet about a pinwheel, especially when adorned in beautiful, pale colors of washi.

WHAT YOU DO

Printing Text on Washi

1 Decide on the text that you'd like to print on washi. Arrange and size the desired text on the computer and use your inkjet printer to print it out onto a piece of translucent vellum.

2 Stick lengths of washi directly over the printed words on the vellum. Make sure that the washi is precisely horizontal and directly over the printed text, blocking out the words.

3 Lightly sand the washi and then wipe away the dust from the sanding.

4 Feed the vellum sheet with the washi through the printer and print exactly the same text from step 1 again. You will now have strips of washi with words printed on top.

DESIGNER: Cynthia Shaffer

WHAT YOU'LL NEED

Basic Washi Kit, page 9
Washi:
- Light pink, standard
- Light purple, standard
- Dotted purple, standard

Computer and inkjet printer
1 sheet of translucent vellum
Fine-grit sandpaper
Sheets of deli paper, 4 inches (10.2 cm) square, one per pinwheel
Hole punch, 1/16-inch (1.6 mm)
Straight pin
Pink and purple mini metal brads, one per pinwheel
Pink plastic straws, one for each pinwheel with a handle
6-strand purple embroidery floss
Translucent gift envelopes (optional)
Gift boxes, various sizes
White butcher paper
1 sheet of transparency film

happy BABY sHower ... Mellisa

Can't WAIT to MEeT YOU !

WelCome Baby Aguilar

Make the Pinwheels

1 Stick strips of washi along all four sides of one of the 4-inch (10.2 cm) deli paper squares. Allow the washi strips to overlap at the corners (fig. A).

2 Fold the deli paper in half diagonally and then open it back up. Fold it again in the opposite direction and open it back up. The deli paper should now have an X-shaped crease mark that makes four equally shaped triangles.

3 Cut into each of the folded marks approximately two-thirds of the way toward the center on each folded mark.

4 With the washi-covered side facing you, punch a small hole into the top left corner of each triangle (fig. B).

5 From the back, poke a hole into the center of the deli paper with a straight pin (fig. C).

6 With the washi-covered side facing you, insert a mini brad into the hole of just one of the triangles. Bring the next triangle up to the brad and insert the brad into the hole. Repeat for the remaining two triangles and then insert the mini brad into the hole at the center of the deli paper and splay out the back brad tabs to secure the pinwheel* (fig. D).

If the pinwheel is going on a straw for one of the gifts, punch a small hole into the top of a straw and insert the mini brad from step 6 into the straw before splaying out the back brad tabs (fig. E).

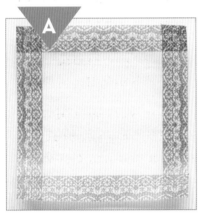

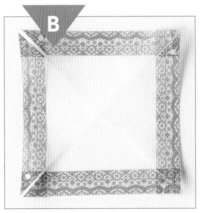

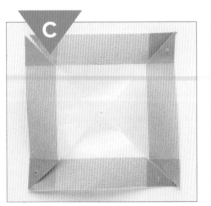

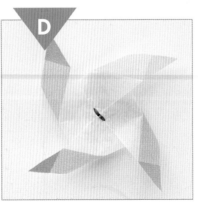

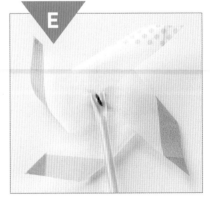

Make the Pinwheel Garland

1 Follow steps 1 through 6 from Pinwheels to make seven pinwheels with assorted coordinating washi colors and patterns.

2 With the right side facing you, punch a small hole at the very top point of one of the pinwheel tips. Repeat for all seven pinwheels.

3 Push all strands of the embroidery floss through the hole on one of the pinwheels and tie a loose knot. Repeat this step until all pinwheels are knotted onto the floss (fig. F).

Make the Gift Bags

1 Use premade translucent envelopes or make your own by folding pieces of deli paper around your gift and taping it securely with washi.

2 Place pinwheels with straws on top of the gift bags and secure them with pieces of washi or washi with text (fig. G).

Make the Gift Boxes

1 Place gifts in boxes and wrap them with white butcher paper.

2 Stick strips of washi onto the smaller box, including a strip with text. Stick a strip of washi onto the transparency and punch out small circles. Remove the washi circles from the transparency and stick them onto one of the washi pieces on the gift box (fig. H).

3 Stick strips of washi onto the larger box, including a strip of washi with text. Wrap the 6-strand embroidery floss several times around the box, tie, and trim (fig. I).

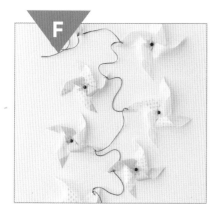

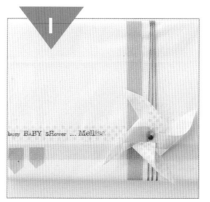

flower-topped GIFTS

DESIGNER: Anne Stills

WHAT YOU'LL NEED

Basic Washi Kit, page 9
Washi: assorted colors and patterns, standard and thick
White cardstock for a 2-inch (5.1 cm) circle
1 decorative button per flower
Strong-bonding glue
14 to 18 small peel-and-stick rhinestones per flower
Boxed gift
White butcher paper

Washi flowers add sparkle to a wrapped gift, and individually folded petals allow for complete personalization of palettes and patterns. Instructions are for one flower, but you'll want to make more!

WHAT YOU DO

1 Cut a 2-inch (5.1 cm) circle from cardstock. It doesn't have to be perfect; this will be the base of the flower and will be entirely covered up.

2 Tear a piece of thick washi approximately 3 inches (7.6 cm) long. Lay it horizontally on your work surface, sticky side up. Find the center of the strip, and fold down the left end at a 45-degree angle until the tape sticks to itself. Repeat with the right end (fig. A on page 66).

3 Rotate the left end over the right end at a 45-degree angle so they stick together to create a flower petal. Stick the petal to the outer edge of the paper circle (fig. B on page 66).

4 Repeat steps 1 through 3 until the entire circumference of the paper circle is covered with washi flower petals. Allow the petals to overlap slightly (fig. C).

5 Switch to a standard washi and repeat steps 1 through 3, sticking the finished petals slightly more toward the center of the paper circle and hiding the loose edges of the first layer of petals (fig. D).

6 Switch to another color of standard washi and repeat steps 1 through 3, sticking the petals in the center of the paper circle, hiding the loose edges of the second layer of petals (fig. E).

7 Glue a decorative button to the center of the flower, hiding the loose edges of washi from the third set of petals. Attach small peel-and-stick rhinestones around the decorative button, spaced evenly apart.

8 Wrap a boxed gift with white butcher paper. Wrap long strips of washi around the wrapped gift to create decorative patterns (fig. F).

9 Glue a completed washi flower to the top of the wrapped gift (fig. G).

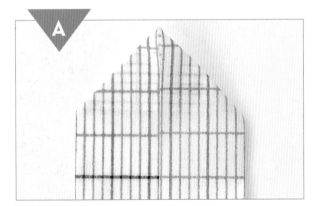

A

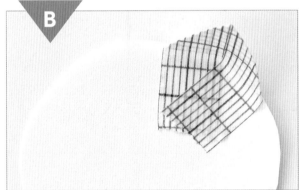

B

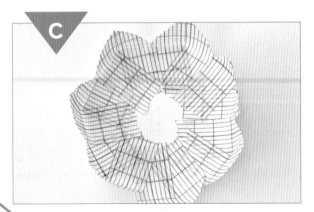

C

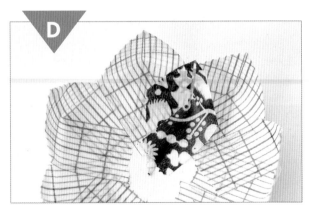

D

WASHI WONDERFUL

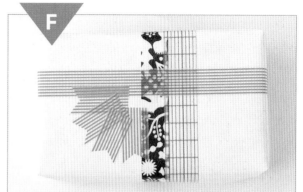

IDEAS

* Instead of buttons, glue photos of gift recipients inside flowers.

* Experiment with the spacing of petals and the numbers of rows to get a fuller or thinner flower.

* Glue a flat magnet to the back of the flower before affixing it to the gift. Tape a small piece of sheet metal to the gift to allow the magnetic flower to stay temporarily on the gift.

homemade
GIFT WRAP

Turn your favorite washi tapes into unlimited wrapping paper by making copies! Then attach dimensional embellishments, such as pom-poms and bows, for added interest.

WHAT YOU DO

The Paper

1 Stick strips of washi in assorted colors, patterns, and thicknesses onto one side of a piece of plain white printer paper. Stick the strips side by side or in any other direction and pattern that you like.

2 Make color copies of the washi-covered paper, a few sheets at 100 percent and a few sheets enlarged to 200 percent.

3 Wrap the boxed gifts in the color copies. Alternatively, wrap one box in white butcher paper and then one of the color copies for a multi-layered wrapped look.

The Embellishments

1 To create a string pom-pom:

* Wrap approximately 24 inches (61 cm) of cotton twine around the cardboard square (fig. A on page 70).
* Carefully slide the wrapped twine off the cardboard (fig. B on page 70).
* Tightly tie the center with a 12-inch (30.5 cm) piece of twine so that it looks like a large bow with lots of loops on each side (fig. C on page 70).

DESIGNER: Anne Stills

WHAT YOU'LL NEED

Basic Washi Kit, page 9
Washi: assorted patterns and colors, standard and thick
White printer paper
Access to a color copier
Boxed gifts in assorted sizes
White butcher paper
5 pieces of white cotton twine:
  * Two 24-inch (61 cm) long pieces
  * Three 12-inch (30.5 cm) long pieces
1 piece of cardboard, 2 inches square (5.1 cm)
White plastic grocery sack
Alphabet stamps
Black permanent inkpad

* Cut all the loops open to make a pom-pom. Unwind each strand of twine to give it a frayed look (fig. D).

2 Create a string ribbon by repeating step 1 without cutting the loops to make a pompom. Instead, tie the string ribbon to the gift.

3 To create a plastic pompom:

* Lay the plastic bag flat on your work surface with the plastic handles on the right side and the bag's bottom on the left side. Cut up the bag from bottom to top to make 1-inch (2.5 cm) wide strips.
* Stack the strips flat, lined up on top of each other.

* Fold the stack in half twice. Tie the middle of the folded strips with a 12-inch (30.5 cm) piece of twine (fig. E).
* Cut open the plastic loops on each side and trim the edges of the pom-pom to shape (fig. F).

4 Create and attach washi trumpets as follows:

* Roll a 2-inch (5.1 cm) piece of washi with the sticky side facing in and slightly off-center, so it starts narrow and then gets wider as it rolls onto itself. Repeat this step to create six small washi trumpets (fig. G).

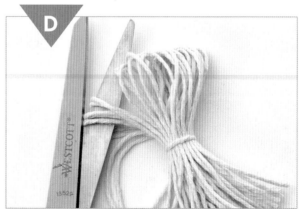

* Glue each trumpet to a small piece of paper with the narrow parts close together at one end. Trim the excess paper. Glue this to the gift and then wrap cotton twine close to the narrow section of the trumpets and make a bow (fig. H).

5 For the text, stick strips of washi onto the cutting mat and stamp holiday messages onto the strips with alphabet stamps and the black permanent inkpad. Stick a stamped strip of washi onto each gift.

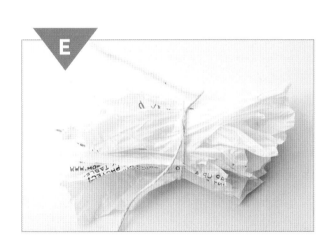

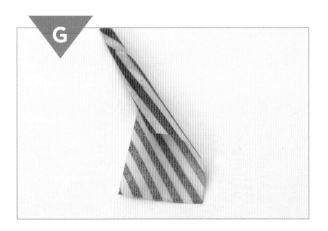

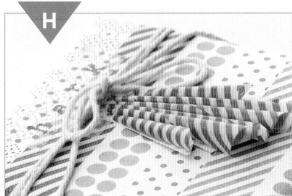

fringes and
TASSELS

It's easy to make your gifts look groovy and chic. Just add a touch of fringe made with colorful combinations of washi!

WHAT YOU DO

Package #1

1 Wrap a gift with newsprint paper. This particular gift measures 10 x 8 x 2 inches (25.4 x 20.3 x 5.1 cm).

2 Place one sheet of translucent vellum on your work surface horizontally. Stick a strip of orange standard washi along one long side of the vellum, ¼ inch (6 mm) from the edge. Place the vellum onto the cutting mat and cut along one edge of the washi, leaving the ¼-inch (6mm) white edge on the opposite side (fig. A on page 74).

3 Cut the washi portion of the strip with fringe scissors, stopping where the vellum starts.

4 With the wrong side facing you, roll the washi vellum fringe. Do this by tightly squeezing and rolling the ¼-inch (6 mm) vellum section onto itself (fig. B).

5 Once the entire strip is rolled up, tape one end on a side edge of the box and carefully pull the inner section out of the roll and across the box to the other side. Tape this end to the box before you let go of the strip, or the twists will come undone (fig. C).

DESIGNER: Jenny Doh

WHAT YOU'LL NEED

Basic Washi Kit, page 9
Washi:
- Orange, standard
- Mint green, thin
- Purple, standard
- Green, standard
- Blue, thin
- Pink, standard
- Cream, standard
- Yellow, thin and standard
- Gray, standard
- Tan, standard

Newsprint paper for wrapping
3 sheets of translucent vellum
Circle paper punch: one ½ inch (1.3 cm) and one 1 inch (2.5 cm)
Fringe scissors*
Shipping tags
Black liquid ink
Small paintbrush
Double-sided tape
Small twigs
Hemp string

* If you don't have fringe scissors, you can use regular scissors to make multiple cuts.

3

xoxo

♡ ♡ ♡

2

love

happy
birthday

1

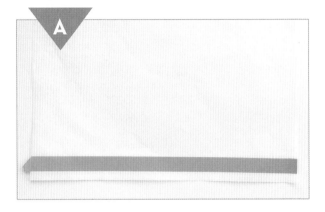

6 Stick another strip of orange washi onto the translucent vellum. Stick a strip of mint green washi onto the vellum, butted right next to the orange washi. Punch small circles out of the taped vellum piece.

7 Remove the punched circles from the vellum and stick them onto the gift. Stick additional strips of orange and mint green washi onto the package (fig. D).

8 Write "happy birthday" with the small paintbrush and black liquid ink onto a shipping tag and let it dry. Stick this onto the gift with more washi.

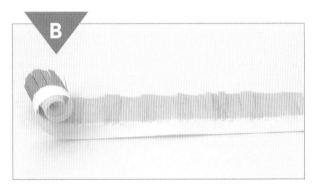

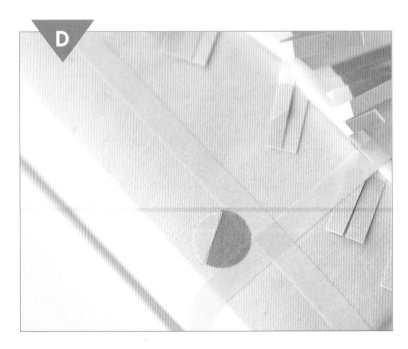

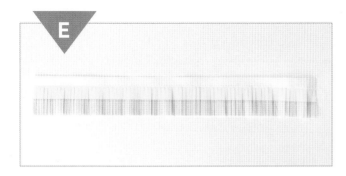

Package #2

1 Wrap a gift with newsprint paper. This particular gift measures 4 x 7 x 2 inches (10.2 x 17.8 x 5.1 cm).

2 Repeat steps 2 and 3 from Package #1, but stick one purple strip and one green strip of washi close together (fig. E).

3 With the wrong side facing you, adhere double-sided tape to the ¼-inch (6 mm) vellum edge. Tightly squeeze and roll the taped vellum section onto itself (fig. F).

4 Wrap hemp string around the top of the tassel, right where the double-sided tape ends and the ¼-inch vellum begins. Tie it tightly into a double knot.

5 Repeat steps 2 through 4 to make a second tassel.

6 Place the two tassels on top of the gift and stick strips of washi onto the tassels' strings to secure them in place. Stick additional strips of washi on the gift (fig. G).

7 Tear a piece of a shipping tag into a small strip and write "love" on it with the small paintbrush and black liquid ink. Let it dry. Stick it onto the gift with small strips of blue washi.

Package #3

1 Wrap a gift with newsprint paper. This particular gift measures 6 x 5 x 5 inches (15.2 x 12.7 x 12.7 cm).

2 Repeat steps 2 and 3 from Package #1 with a strip of gray washi and a strip of pink washi (fig. H).

3 With the right side of the pink washi fringe facing you, adhere double-sided tape to the ¼-inch (6 mm) vellum edge. Place the back side of the gray vellum edge onto the double-sided tape. You now have a double washi fringe strip (fig. I).

4 Stick a yellow thin strip of washi to the center of the double washi fringe strip. Adhere the double washi fringe strip to the top of the gift and stick additional strips of washi to the sides of the gift.

5 Stick strips of gray standard washi onto translucent vellum, allowing the strips to slightly overlap. Punch large circles out of the taped vellum.

6 Peel the circles off of the vellum and stick them onto the gift in a random fashion.

7 Tear a shipping tag into smaller pieces. Write "XOXO" on one piece and draw three hearts on a second piece with the small paintbrush and black liquid ink. Let them dry. Stick it onto the gift with strips of washi.

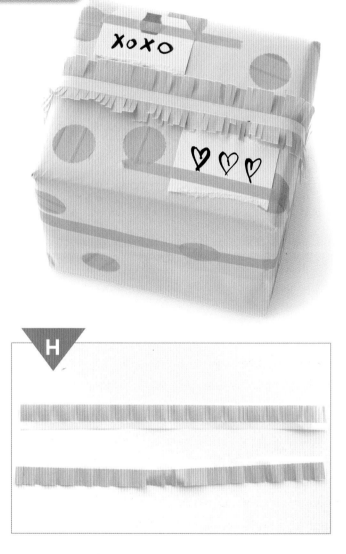

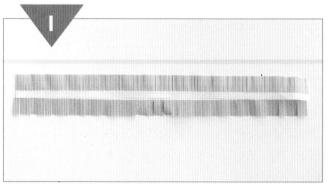

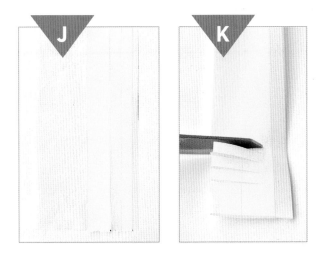

Package #4

1 Wrap a gift with newsprint paper. This particular gift measures 3¾ x 6¾ x 2 inches (9.5 x 17.1 x 5.1 cm).

2 Place a sheet of translucent vellum on your work surface horizontally. Stick a piece of yellow washi along one long side of the vellum, ¼ inch (6 mm) from the edge. Stick three additional pieces of yellow washi abutted close to one another (fig. J).

3 Place the vellum onto the cutting mat and cut the vellum ¼ inch (6 mm) away from the fourth strip, to leave a white edge on both sides of the cut piece.

4 Fold the taped vellum strip at the center, between the second and third washi strips. Adhere the vellum edges with double-sided tape. Cut across the entire folded edge, with fringe or regular scissors, stopping where the ¼ inch (6 mm) of vellum starts (fig. K).

5 Adhere double-sided tape to the ¼-inch (6 mm) vellum edge. Stick one end of the folded fringe onto a twig and wrap it around repeatedly until the entire fringe is on the twig to form a flower (fig. L).

6 Wrap a piece of hemp string around the fringe-wrapped twig and make a bow.

7 Attach the fringe twig flower to the gift with pieces of washi.

8 Tear a shipping tag into a smaller piece and make small dots on it with the small paintbrush and black liquid ink. Let it dry. Stick this piece onto the gift with pieces of washi.

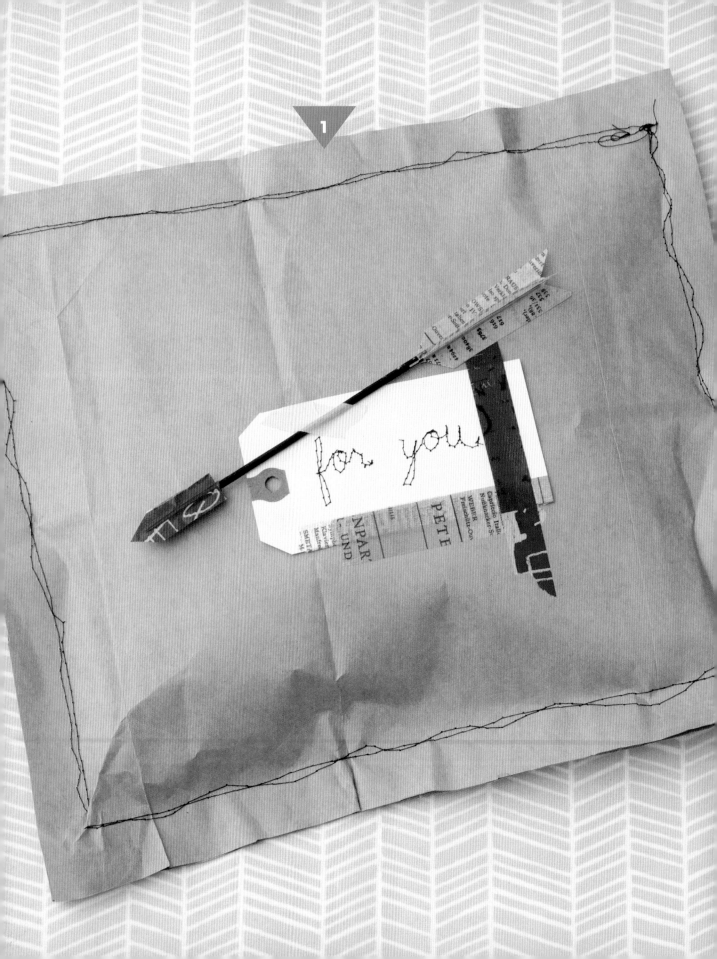

arrow GIFT TOPPERS

DESIGNER: Jenny Doh

WHAT YOU'LL NEED

Basic Washi Kit, page 9
Washi:
- Patterned blue, standard
- Patterned red, standard
- Light yellow, standard
- Patterned blue/yellow, standard
- Patterned cream, standard
- Green, standard

Bamboo skewers, 10 inches
(25.4 cm) long
Black matte spray paint

2 brown paper grocery bags
Sewing machine with darning foot
Black thread
Shipping tags
Gift box
Hemp string
Black liquid ink
Small paintbrush
1 empty paper towel roll
Alphabet stamps
Black inkpad

Pieces of washi are adhered to bamboo skewers for these clever arrows. Attach them to a hand-wrapped gift for added character.

WHAT YOU DO

Arrows

1 Cut 2 inches (5.1 cm) off of the blunt end of a bamboo skewer with sharp scissors. Spray the bamboo skewer with black spray paint and let it dry (fig. A on page 80).

2 Tear patterned blue washi into a piece approximately 3½ inches (8.9 cm) long. Stick this onto the cut end of the bamboo skewer, allowing one end to extend slightly beyond the end of the skewer. Don't wrap the washi around the skewer. Let the skewer lie flat in the center of the washi piece.

3 Tear a piece of patterned red washi approximately 2 inches (5.1 cm) long and stick it on the pointed end of the skewer.

4 Tear a second piece of red washi the same length as the first and press it flat on the sticky side of the red washi with the skewer sandwiched in between.

5 Tear a second piece of patterned blue washi the same length as the first. But this time, don't press it flat against the first piece; instead, align long edges on one side and leave the other edge folded up and away from the skewer. Tear a third piece of blue washi the same length and press it onto the sticky portions of the first and second piece. These will be the arrow's vanes (fig. B).

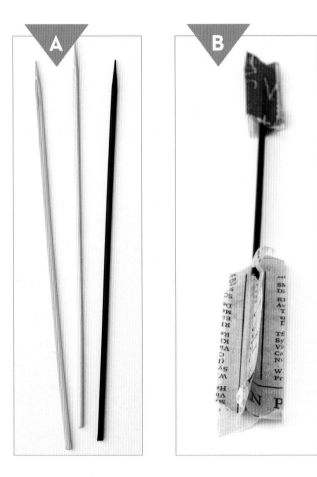

6 Trim the bottom of the washi vanes with scissors to make inverted V shapes. Trim the top of the vanes at an angle to match.

7 Trim the top of the patterned red washi pieces into a V shape. Trim the opposite end of the red washi layers straight across. This will be the point of the arrow (fig. C and D).

8 Repeat steps 1 through 7 to make additional arrows with assorted colors and patterns of washi.

Package #1

1 Cut a brown paper grocery bag into two pieces, approximately 12½ x 11 inches (31.8 x 27.9 cm) each.

2 Prepare your sewing machine to free-motion stitch by attaching the darning foot and lowering the feed dogs. Free-motion stitch one short side, then one long side, and then the second short side to create a pocket. Insert the gift into the pocket and free-motion stitch the final side closed.

3 Free-motion stitch the words "for you" on a shipping tag.

4 Attach a washi arrow onto the top of the tag with a light yellow piece of washi. Attach the tag with the washi arrow to the center of the gift with strips of patterned red and blue washi.

Package #2

1 Cut a brown paper grocery bag into a piece large enough to wrap your gift box. Insert the gift into the box and wrap it.

2 Wrap the box with hemp string several times horizontally and tie in place.

3 Write "XOXO" with black liquid ink and a small paintbrush on a shipping tag and let it dry.

4 Insert the tag and a washi arrow between the layers of wrapped string.

Package #3

1 Cut a brown paper grocery bag large enough to wrap the empty paper towel roll. Insert the gift into the roll and wrap it with the paper.

2 Stamp the words "BE MINE" onto a shipping tag and tear off part of the shipping tag. Attach the tag to the gift with green washi.

3 Place a washi arrow on top of the tag. Wrap the gift, tag, and washi arrow several times with hemp string and tie them in place. Make a bow.

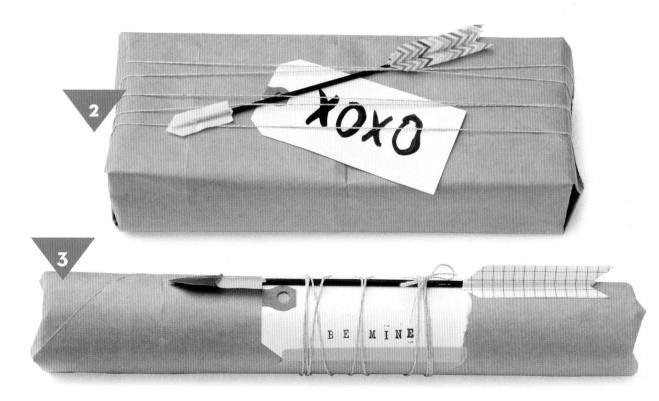

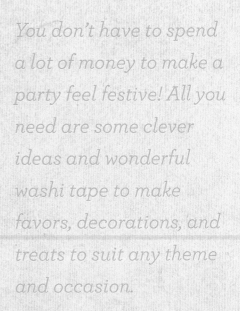

You don't have to spend a lot of money to make a party feel festive! All you need are some clever ideas and wonderful washi tape to make favors, decorations, and treats to suit any theme and occasion.

butterfly GARLAND

This delicate butterfly banner would fit perfectly in front of a window in a little girl's room, or as a cheerful decoration for a butterfly-themed birthday party or backyard gathering.

DESIGNER: Ishtar Olivera Belart

WHAT YOU'LL NEED

Basic Washi Kit, page 9
Washi: Assorted patterned
   purples, pinks, and greens,
   standard
White cardstock cut
   into several 3-inch
   (7.6 cm) squares
Butterfly-shaped paper punch,
   2 inches (5.1 cm) wide

White acrylic paint
Small paintbrush
Transparent tape
Double-sided tape
Baker's twine, 3 yards
   (2.7 m)

WHAT YOU DO

1 Stick strips of washi onto a cardstock square, allowing the strips to slightly overlap. You can use just one type of washi or several different kinds (fig. A).

2 Punch a butterfly out of the washi-covered cardstock (fig. B). Repeat this process to make a second washi butterfly shape (fig. C). Leave the butterfly shapes as they are or add details with white acrylic paint and the small paintbrush. Let dry.

3 Starting at one end of the baker's twine, tape the twine to the wrong side of one of the butterfly shapes.

Adhere the wrong side of the second butterfly shape onto the wrong side of the first butterfly shape with double-sided tape (fig. D).

4 Repeat steps 1 through 3 until you have attached 22 butterflies (or as many as you need for your desired length of garland). Be sure to leave approximately 2 inches (5.1 cm) in between each butterfly. In the space between butterflies, fold a strip of washi onto the baker's twine and then cut out a V shape on the outer edge.

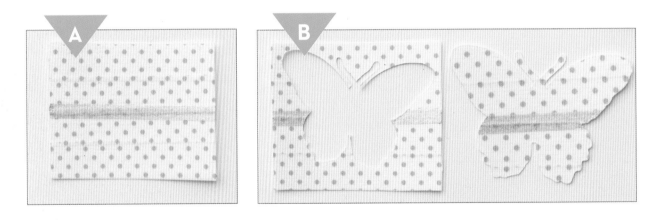

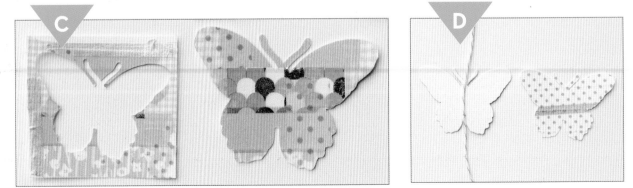

sweet TREATS

Designer: Carolyn Garris

Creative Idea #1: Cut craft wire into 3-inch (7.6 cm) pieces. Place a wire lengthwise on the sticky side of a piece of washi and fold the washi to encase the wire. Trim both ends with scissors. Repeat this to make several more washi wire twists. Wrap candies with pieces of clear cellophane and twist the ends with the washi wire twists.

Creative Idea #2: Wrap candy with pieces of parchment paper and wrap a piece of washi around the parchment to secure. Twist both ends.

paper plate FAVOR BOXES

Every good party needs favors. Made from colorful paper plates and washi to match the party's color scheme, these favor boxes filled with treats are sure to be a hit.

DESIGNER: Ishtar Olivera Belart

WHAT YOU'LL NEED

Basic Washi Kit, page 9
Washi:
- Hot pink, standard and thick
- Assorted colors, patterns, and widths

Colored paper plates*
Scallop-edged paper punch
White cardstock
Wooden craft sticks

Computer and printer
White copy paper

* *You can use any size of paper plates you'd like to make larger or smaller boxes. The ones shown for this project measure approximately 7 inches (17.8 cm) in diameter.*

WHAT YOU DO

Box #1

1 Sketch a cross shape on the back of a paper plate and cut it out (fig. A).

2 Stick a hot pink piece of washi on one of the outer edges of the plate, colored side up (fig. B).

3 Punch the edge with a scallop-edged paper punch (fig. C).

4 Repeat steps 2 and 3 with the other three outer edges.

5 Fold up the four sections of the plate so the colored side is on the outside, and hold the sections together with strips of washi in assorted colors, patterns, and widths (fig. D).

Box #2

1 Sketch a cross shape on the back of a paper plate and cut it out.

2 Fold the four sections of the plate up so the colored side is on the inside, and hold the sections together with strips of washi in assorted colors, patterns, and widths.

Craft Stick Signs

1 Stick pieces of washi tape in assorted colors, patterns, and widths onto white cardstock. Cut the cardstock into circles, rectangles, or other desired shapes.

2 Use a computer and printer to generate names of guests (or a quote or other fun text) onto white copy paper and cut out each name in the shape of a small flag with a V shape at one end. Attach the cutouts to the prepared cardstock shapes using thin pieces of washi.

3 Attach wooden craft sticks to the backs of the prepared shapes with washi.

4 Fill the boxes with treats and use the treats to hold up the signs.

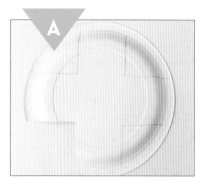

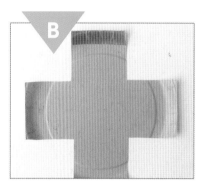

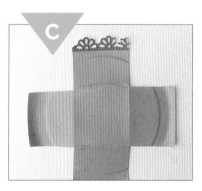

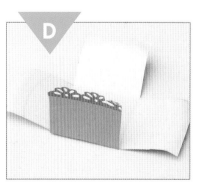

pretty little MATCHBOXES

Empty matchboxes become treasured trinket holders or secret note keepers with strips of washi, a few rubber stamps, and your imagination.

DESIGNER: Ishtar Olivera Belart

WHAT YOU'LL NEED

Basic Washi Kit, page 9
Washi:
- Patterned red, standard
- Dotted navy, standard
- Patterned purple, standard
- Patterned blue, standard

Empty matchboxes, 1½ x 2 x ⅝ inches (3.8 x 5.1 x 1.6 cm)
Stickers (optional)
Small heart-shaped paper punch
Assorted paper scraps
Glue stick
Rubber stamps with a tea theme
Gray inkpad
Red and black fine-point markers
House template (see page 141)
1 sheet of cardstock

WHAT YOU DO

Matchbox #1

1 Separate the interior and exterior portions of the matchbox so you can embellish them separately. Start by covering the inside bottom of the interior piece with strips of red washi. This process does not have to be precise. Uneven ends are okay and strips placed horizontally, vertically, and even diagonally are okay. If you want, add more washi strips to cover the inside walls of the interior piece.

2 Attach strips of washi to the underside of the interior piece. If you want, attach washi to all the outer edges of the interior piece, allowing the washi to overlap as needed. If the washi is thicker than the edges, fold the excess over or trim it with scissors.

3 Using the same concept, cover the exterior portion of the matchbox with strips of dotted navy washi. Fold under any excess tape or trim the excess with scissors. (For this box, I deliberately cut strips of washi into irregular pieces and attached them to the box without overlapping them so parts of the matchbox would show through.) Attach a sticker to the exterior.

4 Punch tiny hearts from assorted patterned paper scraps and place them in the matchbox.

Matchbox #2

1 Repeat steps 1 and 2 of Matchbox #1 to embellish the matchbox interior. (I used washi with a purple checked pattern.)

2 For the exterior, cut a piece of patterned paper that measures 1½ x 2 inches (3.8 x 5.1 cm) and adhere it to the top of the box with a glue stick. Decorate the edges of the box with patterned red and patterned blue washi. Cut a scalloped edge on one of the red washi strips before attaching it to the box. Attach a tea-themed sticker.

3 Stamp tea-themed images with a gray inkpad onto white cardstock and cut them out. Embellish the cutouts with small pieces of red patterned washi, and add doodles with red and black fine-point markers.

Matchbox #3

1 Repeat steps 1 and 2 of Matchbox #1 to embellish the matchbox interior. (I used washi with a blue checked pattern on the ends only.)

2 Stick dotted red washi to the outside edges of matchbox exterior.

3 Trace the house template onto cardstock and cut it out. Decorate the house shape with dotted red washi, patterned blue washi and other embellishments.

4 Attach the decorated house piece to the top of the matchbox with a glue stick.

wooden ball PARTY FAVORS

Designer: Carolyn Garris

Creative Idea: Stick strips of washi onto a self-healing mat. Use a ruler and sharp craft knife to cut the strips into halves, thirds, or even fourths to make them narrower. Also, depending on the pattern of the washi, cut out interesting shapes and designs inspired by the washi that you are using. Stick the strips and shapes onto the wooden balls however you like.

stars and stripes
MASON JAR GLASSES

DESIGNER: Cynthia Shaffer

Decorated glasses for a summer celebration set a playful tone. Add a fun striped straw, and it's time to party!

WHAT YOU'LL NEED

Basic Washi Kit, page 9
Washi:
- Dotted red, standard
- Patterned blue, standard
- Light blue, standard
- Patterned red, standard
- Light yellow, thin

5 Mason jars with two-part lids, 8-ounce size
1 sheet of transparency film
Black fine-point permanent marker
Star template (see page 141)
Scissors
Hole punch
5 striped paper straws

WHAT YOU DO

1 Remove the inner solid circle part of the lid from all the Mason jars. Trace one of the inner solid circles five times on the transparency with the black permanent marker. Set the inner solid circle parts of the lids aside (fig. A on the next page).

2 Adhere strips of washi in various colors and patterns onto one of the traced circles, allowing the tape to overlap as much as you want (see Vellum Method on page 12). Make sure that the washi extends slightly beyond the circle. Repeat this step for all the traced circles.

3 Use the marker's tracings as a guide to cut out all the circles with scissors.

4 Trace the star template five times on the transparency with a black permanent marker (fig. B).

5 Stick small strips of dotted red washi onto one of the stars, allowing the strips to slightly overlap one another. Make sure that the washi extends slightly beyond the star. Repeat this step for all the traced stars (fig. C).

6 Cut out all the stars with scissors, using the marker's tracings as a guide.

7 Punch a hole at the center of each of the cutout stars. Also punch a hole slightly off-center on each of the cutout circles (fig. D).

8 Slip a straw through one of the stars and then through one of the washi inner lids. Fill the Mason jar with a beverage and then pop the washi inner lid under the outer lid and screw the outer lid onto the Mason jar. Repeat this step for all the jars (fig. E).

A

B

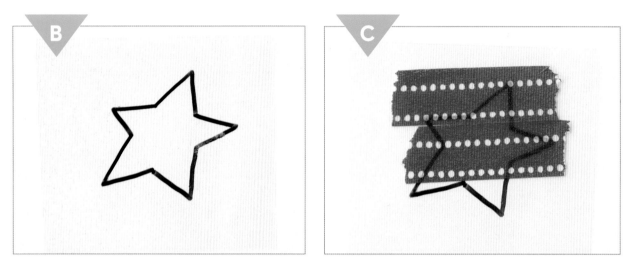

C

D

E

WASHI WONDERFUL

embellished EGGS

If you're not in the mood to dye eggs this year, decorate them with washi instead. Tiny pieces of washi become endearing neighborhood scenes on these charming eggs.

DESIGNER: Cynthia Shaffer

WHAT YOU'LL NEED

Basic Washi Kit, page 9
Washi:
- Blue, standard
- Light blue, standard
- Green, standard
- Yellow-green, standard
- Brown, standard
- Tan, standard

3 hard-boiled eggs
Bone folder
Black fine-point permanent marker
1 sheet of transparency film

WHAT YOU DO

Egg #1

1 Tear pieces of blue, light blue, and medium green washi into strips about ½ to ¾ inches (1.3 to 1.9 cm) long. Stick these pieces onto a hard-boiled egg, spaced slightly apart. Smooth out small wrinkles in the washi pieces with a bone folder.

2 Cut straight across the torn edges with the sharp craft knife, and remove the excess washi. These pieces will be the house shapes.

3 Tear off small pieces of brown and patterned tan washi, about ½ to ¾ inch (1.3 to 1.9 cm) long, one for each house. Stick one above each house, overlapping the house shape slightly.

4 Cut diagonally on both sides of each brown washi piece with the sharp craft knife to create roofs for the houses. Some can be pointed and some can be squared off.

5 Stick small pieces of washi in assorted colors onto the cutting mat and cut tiny squares and triangles with the sharp craft knife. Stick these onto the houses for doors and windows.

6 Stick a 4-inch (10.2 cm) piece of yellow-green washi onto the cutting mat. Make little cuts about ⅛ inch (3 mm) apart widthwise into the washi. Be careful not to cut through to the top of the washi.

7 Carefully peel the washi off the cutting mat and stick it onto the bottom portion of the egg, spreading the little sections as you work your way around the bottom. This will be the grass. Repeat with blue washi for the top of the egg.

8 Draw small details such as doorknobs and windowpanes directly on the washi pieces with a black fine-point permanent marker.

Egg #2

1 Tear small pieces of washi in a variety of browns and tans and stick them on the cutting mat. Cut them into small rectangles in varying widths and heights with the sharp craft knife. Stick these onto the egg, spaced slightly apart. These will be the tree trunks. Smooth out small wrinkles in the washi pieces with a bone folder.

2 Tear off small pieces of washi in assorted greens and stick them onto a sheet of transparency. Cut the transparency-covered washi into circles and ovals for the tree tops.

3 Peel the washi circles and ovals off the transparency and stick them above the tree trunks.

4 Repeat steps 6 and 7 from Egg #1 to add washi grass.

5 Draw small details such as leaves and dots on the tree tops with a black fine-point permanent marker.

Egg #3

1 Tear off two pieces of blue washi and stick them on the cutting mat. Cut them into rectangles with a sharp craft knife, making one rectangle slightly smaller.

2 Stick these rectangle pieces onto the center of the egg, overlapping them just a little to make the shape look like a two-sided house. Smooth out small wrinkles in the washi pieces with a bone folder.

3 Tear off two small pieces of brown washi and stick them on the cutting mat. Cut them into roof shapes with the sharp craft knife. Adhere them above the house shape.

4 Repeat steps 1 through 3 from Egg #2 to make small trees next to the house.

5 Repeat steps 6 and 7 from Egg #1 to add washi grass.

6 Draw small details such as doorknobs, windowpanes, and leaves on the house and trees with a black fine-point permanent marker.

friendship CUPCAKE PICKS

There's nothing cuter than a cupcake—except maybe a cupcake with a topper! These cupcake picks are made from shipping tags and can be thrown together in a jiffy for any celebration.

DESIGNER: Jenny Doh

WHAT YOU'LL NEED

Basic Washi Kit, page 9
Washi: assorted coordinating colors, widths, and patterns
Shipping tags, 2½ x 4¾ inches (6.4 x 12 cm)

Small photographs
Heart-shaped paper punch, 1¼ inches (3.2 cm)
Toothpicks
Strong-bonding glue

WHAT YOU DO

1 Tear washi in assorted patterns and colors, into pieces slightly longer than 2½ inches (6.4 cm) each. Stick a strip horizontally across the bottom edge of the shipping tag, followed by another color, then another color, until the tag is covered.

2 Punch out a heart shape from the shipping tag. Save both the heart-shaped piece and the punched tag (fig. A).

3 Repeat steps 1 and 2 to make a second heart shape identical to the first.

4 Squeeze a tiny bit of strong-bonding glue to the wrong side of one of the hearts. Place one end of a toothpick into the glue and then place the second washi heart on top. Let it dry on a flat surface (fig. B).

5 Cut the top and bottom edges of the punched tag from step 2 with scallop-edged scissors. Trim the left and right sides with scissors so the tag measures 1⅝ inches (4.1 cm) square. This will be the washi frame.

6 Cut a photograph to fit behind the washi frame.

7 Apply a layer of spray adhesive to the back side of the washi frame. Place it on top of the right side of the photo, centering the photo in the cutout hole.

8 Cut a shipping tag to measure slightly smaller than the washi frame.

9 Squeeze a tiny bit of strong-bonding glue onto the cut tag. Place one end of a toothpick into the glue and then place the washi frame on top. Let this dry on a flat surface (fig. C).

10 Repeat steps 1 through 9 with assorted colors of washi to create additional cupcake picks.

IDEA

On some tags, leave space between some of the washi strips to allow some of the tag to show through. Use that space to add doodles or a guest's name.

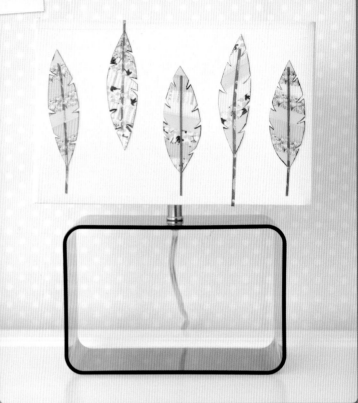

Beyond cards, gift wrap, and party décor is a whole host of diverse projects that can be made with washi tape. So gather your rolls of washi to make jewelry, jars, lamps, and more!

sweet and scalloped
PANTRY JAR LABELS

Storing pantry goods
in recycled glass
jars is an effective
upcycling method.
With scalloped washi
and inventive labels,
it can be a cute
method, too!

DESIGNER: Cynthia Shaffer

WHAT YOU'LL NEED

Basic Washi Kit, page 9
Washi: brown, standard
4 recycled jars in assorted
   sizes and shapes
Computer and inkjet printer
1 sheet of translucent vellum
1 sheet of transparency film

Scallop-edged paper punch
Double-sided tape
Clear packing tape, 2 inches
   (5.1 cm) wide
Fine-grit sandpaper
Damp cloth
Black matte spray paint

Oatmeal;
{oht-meel} noun
meal ground from oats, used for making porridge

Sugar;
{shoog-er} noun
1. a sweet, crystalline substance,
obtained chiefly from the juice of the sugar

Brown Sugar;
{broun shoo g-er} noun
unrefined or partially refined sugar
that retains some molasses

Flour;
{flouuh r} noun
1. the finely ground meal of grain

WHAT YOU DO

1 Type up the label text on your computer. Include pronunciations, parts of speech, and definitions, as desired. Make sure the height of the text for each label is not more than 1 inch (2.5 cm): the height of each label needs to be just under 2 inches (5.1 cm) to fit under the packing tape. The widths can vary to fit your chosen jars.

2 Print the text onto translucent vellum using an inkjet printer. Cut the printed vellum into labels with a sharp craft knife, ruler, and self-healing cutting mat (fig. A).

3 Pick the vellum label for the first jar you would like to make and stick a length of brown washi onto a transparency sheet, making sure that the washi is slightly longer than the long side of the vellum label. Punch the entire length of the washi on the transparency with a scallop-edged paper punch (fig. B).

4 Repeat step 3 to make a second piece of washi for the bottom long side of the vellum label.

5 Peel the washi from each transparency and stick it on the top and bottom edges of the vellum label,

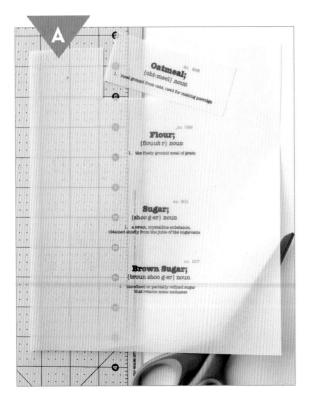

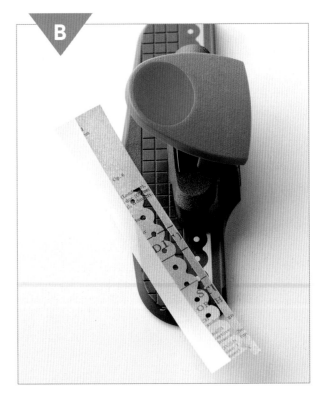

making sure that the washi extends beyond the vellum label on both sides.

6 Adhere the label to the jar with double-sided tape.

7 Stick a length of clear packing tape over the entire label, making sure that the tape extends a little on all sides. Smooth out any wrinkles with your fingers.

8 Repeat steps 3 through 7 with the labels for the other jars.

9 Lightly sand the jar lids with fine-grit sandpaper. Wipe off excess particles with a damp cloth and let dry.

10 Spray the lids with black matte spray paint. Allow them to dry.

11 Fill the jars with their corresponding pantry goods and top them with the painted lids.

bunny *MOBILE*

DESIGNER: Cynthia Shaffer

WHAT YOU'LL NEED

Basic Washi Kit, page 9
Washi:
- Pink, standard
- Light pink, thin
- Patterned pink, standard
- Light orange, standard
- Light blue, standard, thin
- Patterned gray, standard
- Patterned blue, standard
- Light green, standard
- Striped green, standard
- Mint green, thin

Bunny template (page 141)
1 sheet of transparency film
Black fine-point permanent marker
2 sheets of black cardstock
White colored pencil
2 paper clips
Scraps of paper
Spray adhesive
Inner hoop of two-part 6-inch (15.2 cm) wooden embroidery hoop
Black matte spray paint
24-gauge steel wire: four 15-inch (38.1 cm) pieces and one 3-inch (7.6 cm) piece
Needle-nose pliers
Wire cutters
Hole punch, 1/16-inch (1.6 mm)
3 yards of black-and-white baker's twine, cut into 4 equal pieces

Hang this adorable mobile in a child's room, above a crib, or in front of a window. The slightly transparent pieces of washi will catch the sunlight on a golden afternoon, and the black outlines on each bunny add an eye-catching edge.

WHAT YOU DO

1 Trace the bunny template four times onto the transparency sheet with the black permanent marker.

- Adhere assorted shades of pink washi strips onto the transparency sheet, allowing the strips to slightly overlap and extend beyond the marked shape. Repeat this step with the other traced bunny shapes, making one bunny with mostly greens, another with mostly blues, and one with a combination of all colors (see Transparency Method, page 14) (fig. A on page 106).

- Cut out all the washi bunny shapes with scissors, using the marker's tracings as a guide (fig. B).

2 Arrange the four bunny cutouts to fit onto one piece of black cardstock. Trace around all four shapes.

- Place the second sheet of cardstock under the traced cardstock and use paper clips to keep them in place.

- Cut out the bunny shapes through both layers. Keep the cut bunny pairs together.

- Place one pair, stacked on top of one other, on a cutting mat.

* Cut out the inside of the rabbit about ¼ inch (6 mm) from the edge, cutting through both layers. Repeat this step for all four pairs of bunnies (fig. C).

3 Open up one pair of the bunny frames and place them on a piece of scrap paper so the insides of the frames are facing you.

* Spray the insides of the frames with spray adhesive.

* Quickly adhere the front frame to the front of one washi-covered bunny and the back frame to the back side of the same bunny.

* Use a sharp craft knife to cut off any of the bunny edges that might be poking out from the black frames.

* Repeat this step for all four bunnies (fig. D).

4 Generously cover the inner wooden embroidery hoop with black spray paint. Let it dry.

5 Lightly mark the embroidery hoop with the white pencil in four equal distances. To attach the wire:

* Twist the ends of the 15-inch (38.1 cm) wire pieces around the hoop at these marks.

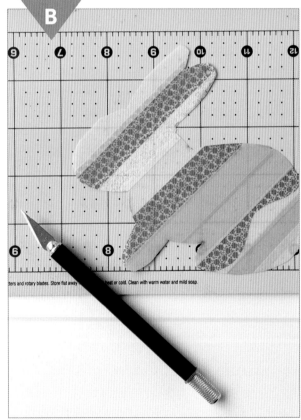

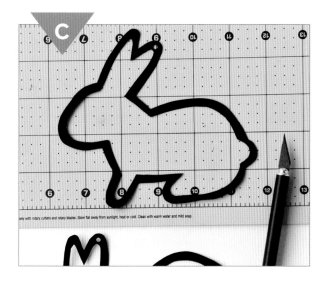

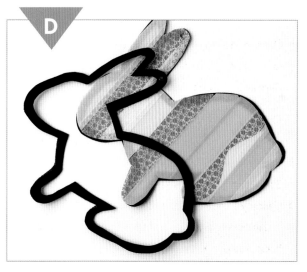

* Twist all four wire pieces together at the top, then use needle-nosed pliers to bend the top ends down to form small loops. Cut any excess wire with the wire cutters.

* Twist the 3-inch (7.6 cm) piece of wire to make a hook that connects the four small loops, with a curve at the top for hanging.

6 Punch small holes in the tip of one bunny ear, for each bunny. Thread baker's twine through these holes and tie each bunny onto the painted hoop at varying lengths (fig. E).

feathered LAMPSHADE

Add feathers—and loads of personality—to a plain lampshade.
Play with the colors and the placement of the feathers for
unique shadows on your walls.

DESIGNER: Cynthia Shaffer

WHAT YOU'LL NEED

Basic Washi Kit, page 9
Washi:
- Blue, standard
- Light yellow, standard
- Dark yellow, standard
- Patterned green/black, standard
- Striped green, standard
- Patterned yellow/green, standard

Feather templates (page 141)
White lampshade,
  11 x 7 x 5 inches
  (27.9 x 17.8 x 12.7 cm)*
1 sheet of transparency film
Black fine-point permanent marker
Double-sided tape

* *This rectangular lampshade
   was purchased at a local retail
   store from the home goods aisle.
   Lampshades of different sizes
   and shapes should work, as long
   as the feather shape can lie flat
   on part of the lampshade.*

WHAT YOU DO

1 Trace the feather templates onto the transparency with the black permanent marker, for a total of 10 feathers (5 of each shape).

2 Adhere strips of washi in various colors and patterns onto one of the traced feather shapes, allowing the strips to slightly overlap and extend beyond the marked shape.

Repeat this step with the other traced feather shapes. Mix up the washi you use and the angle in which you stick it on, so each feather looks unique.

3 Cut out the washi-covered feather shapes with scissors.

4 Outline just the edges of the feathers with the black marker. Use a light hand to keep the outlining subtle and allow some parts to be uneven (fig. A).

5 Adhere the feathers on the lampshade with double-sided tape, in whatever arrangement you like.

6 Stick a 6-inch (15.2 cm) piece of washi onto the cutting mat. Use a ruler and sharp craft knife to cut it into very thin strips. Stick a thin strip down the center of each feather, letting it extend slightly beyond the feather shapes (fig. B).

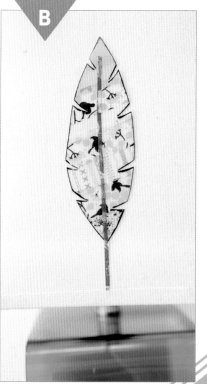

washi fun

WASHI WONDERFUL

origami star
NECKLACE

DESIGNER:
Cynthia Shaffer

WHAT YOU'LL NEED

Basic Washi Kit, page 9
Washi:
- Patterned pink, standard
- Other assorted patterns and colors as desired

1 sheet of translucent vellum
Small beads, pearls, and star charm
Straight pin
Head pin
Needle-nosed pliers
Small beads, pearls, and star charms
Ball chain necklace

With just a strip of washi-covered vellum, you can fold this statement star to wear around your neck. Vary the width of the strip to make the star dainty or bold.

WHAT YOU DO

1 Stick an 11-inch (27.9 cm) length of patterned pink washi on a piece of vellum, aligning the long side of the washi with the long side of the vellum.

2 Cut the vellum along the other long side of the washi with the ruler and the sharp craft knife. You now have a strip of washi-covered vellum that is 11 inches (27.9 cm) long and as wide as the washi.

3 Make a loop with one end of the taped vellum piece as shown (fig. A on next page).

4 Place the short end of the strip through the loop as though you were making a knot, as shown (fig. B).

5 Press the knot down flat, then fold up the short end and tuck it under the fold of the knot. You now have a piece that looks like a small hexagon (fig. C).

6 Fold the other longer end of the strip in the natural direction it wants to go, around and around the hexagon. Tuck the last small bit of the strip into the last folded layer.

7 Place one of the points of the hexagon between your thumb and index finger and pinch it to create one of the star points and slightly fluff and plump up the star's body. Repeat this step for all other points of the hexagon to complete the star (fig. D).

8 Poke a straight pin into the concave section on the bottom of the star and then straight up and out of the star's opposite point. Remove the straight pin.

9 Slip a couple of beads onto a head pin. Insert the head pin into the hole at the bottom and then out the top of the star. Create a small loop in the head pin at the top of the star with needle-nosed pliers. String the star onto a ball chain necklace (fig. E).

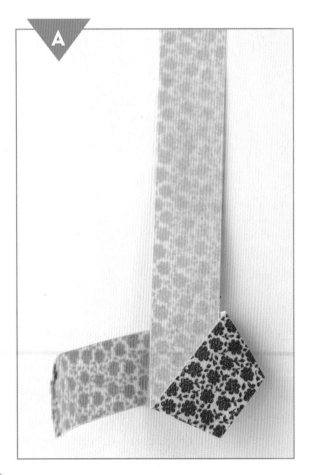

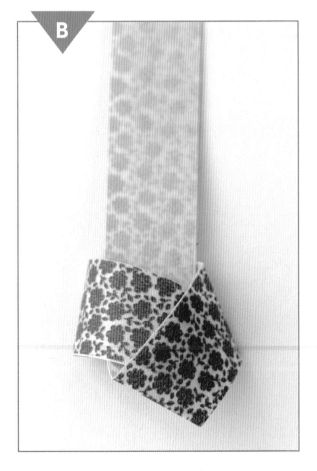

WASHI WONDERFUL

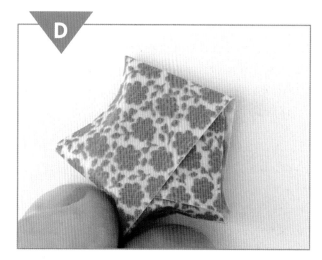

VARIATIONS

* Use a head pin with a loop at the bottom to hang a dangly charm (fig. F).

* Add beads at the top of the star to add more color and length (fig G).

* Use thicker strips of washi-covered vellum to make larger stars and thinner strips of washi-covered vellum to make smaller stars.

embellished

POCKET JOURNALS

Pocket journals are perfect to have on hand for moments of inspiration throughout the day. Tailor your journals to match your personality and preferences for a truly unique record keeper.

DESIGNER: Cynthia Shaffer

WHAT YOU'LL NEED

Basic Washi Kit, page 9
Washi:
- White, standard
- Patterned red, standard
- Patterned dark brown, standard
- Patterned light gray, standard
- Blue, standard

3 small, soft-covered journals, each
  3½ x 5½ inches (8.9 x 14 cm)*
Dotted border paper punch
Sewing machine
Cream and red thread
Scallop-edged paper punch
Hole punch, ¹⁄₁₆ inch (1.6 mm)
4 small metal brads
1 sheet of translucent vellum
Metal alphabet stamps and hammer
Black inkpad
Paper towel

* You can get journals that are larger or
   smaller, but in order to machine stitch
   the covers, make sure you get journals
   with soft covers.

WHAT YOU DO

Journal #1

1 Punch the front right edge of the journal cover with the dotted border paper punch.

2 Stick a 6-inch (15.2 cm) strip of white washi to the front of the journal, about 1 inch (2.5 cm) from the spine. Allow the short edges of the washi to extend beyond the journal. Stick a second 6-inch (15.2 cm) strip of white washi about ¾ inch (1.9 cm) to the right of the first piece of white washi.

3 Stick a 6-inch (15.2 cm) strip of patterned red washi onto the self-healing cutting mat. Cut the washi in half

lengthwise with the ruler and the sharp craft knife. Now you have two thin pieces of red washi.

4 Stick the first piece of thin red washi on top of the first white washi strip from step 2, positioned slightly left of center.

5 Center the second piece of thin red washi in between the two pieces of white washi.

6 Stick a 6-inch (15.2 cm) strip of red washi right on top of the second piece of white washi from step 2, overlapping but positioned slightly to the right.

7 Open up the cover and place it on the cutting mat. Cut the excess washi at the top and bottom of the journal cover with the ruler and the sharp craft knife.

8 Add zigzag and straight stitches with the sewing machine, allowing the stitches to sometimes go through both the washi and the journal cover. Trim hanging threads with scissors.

washi fun

Journal #2

1 Punch the front right edge of the journal cover with the scallop-edged paper punch. Stick a piece of patterned blue washi to the right edge of the first interior page so that the washi shows beneath the scalloped-edged cover.

2 Stick a piece of patterned dark brown washi approximately 2 inches (5.1 cm) long onto the journal cover horizontally, with the right short edge extending slightly beyond the right edge of the cover. Repeat this step with additional pieces of patterned washi in lengths of 1 to 3 inches (2.5 to 7.6 cm). Allow some pieces to overlap each other slightly.

3 Stick a piece of patterned light gray washi onto the cutting mat and cut it in half lengthwise with the ruler and the sharp craft knife. Cut these thin strips into lengths of 1 to 3 inches (2.5 to 7.6 cm) as before and stick them onto the journal cover horizontally. Allow some pieces to overlap one another and some pieces to overlap the washi from step 1.

4 Add horizontal straight stitches with the sewing machine, allowing the stitches to sometimes go through both the washi and the journal cover. Trim hanging threads with scissors.

5 Punch four holes along the right edge of the cover. Attach small metal brads in the holes (fig. A).

A

Journal #3

1 Punch the front right edge of the journal cover with the scallop-edged paper punch.

2 Stick a 6-inch (15.2 cm) strip of blue washi onto the edge of the piece of vellum (see Vellum Method, page 12). Punch the edge of the taped vellum piece with the scallop-edged paper punch.

3 Peel the washi off the vellum and stick it onto the journal cover, with the scallops pointing in the same direction as the punched scallops on the cover.

4 Stick another 6-inch (15.2 cm) strip of blue washi onto the cutting mat, and cut it in half lengthwise with the ruler and the sharp craft knife. Stick one of the halves to the left of the blue scallop on the journal cover.

5 Add zigzag and straight stitches with the sewing machine, allowing the stitches to sometimes go through both the washi and the journal cover.

6 Stamp initials into three of the washi scallops using the metal alphabet stamps and the hammer (fig. B).

7 Rub black ink over the stamped letters with your fingers, and wipe off the excess with the paper towel.

dotted bud vases
WITH CADDY

Convert old glass soda bottles into elegant vases with paint, washi, and darling dots. All you need is a flower—created from washi or picked fresh from your garden—for a dose of instant cheer.

WHAT YOU DO

1 Remove all labels from the soda bottles. Thoroughly wash the bottles inside and out and let them dry.

2 Squeeze a row of silicone dots onto the outside of each soda bottle. Add additional rows of dots as desired, being careful not to smudge any of the dots. If you do smudge a dot, simply wipe the area with the damp paper towel and allow it to dry. Then squeeze a new dot in its place. Allow the dots to thoroughly dry, approximately 45 minutes.

3 Set the bottles on old newspapers in a well-ventilated area (preferably outdoors) and spray paint the outside of the bottles with white spray paint. Let dry.

4 Stick a piece of dotted green washi onto the cutting mat. Using the ruler and sharp craft knife, cut the washi down the center lengthwise so you end up with two thin strips. Cut enough for about 8 thin strips per bottle.

5 Stick the thin strips of washi in varying heights, between the rows of silicone dots. The bottles are now complete (fig. A on page 120).

DESIGNER: Anne Stills

WHAT YOU'LL NEED

Basic Washi Kit, page 9
Washi:
- Dotted green, standard
- Diagonally striped red, standard
- Patterned pink, standard
- Yellow, standard

4 empty glass soda bottles with paper caddy
Silicone in a squeeze tube*
Paper towel
White and green spray paint
Old newspapers
White cardstock
Plastic drinking straw
Strong-bonding glue

* *Silicone that comes in a squeeze tube can be found in home improvement stores.*

6 For the caddy:

* Set the four-pack paper caddy on newspaper and spray it with green spray paint, making sure to cover the entire interior and exterior of the caddy. Let it dry.

* Stick pieces of green patterned washi onto the cutting mat and cut V shapes into one end of each piece. Stick these onto the caddy front, overlapping the edges, so they look like trees.

* Stick a piece of red patterned washi along all the bottom edges of the caddy (covering the bottom of the "trees" in front).

7 To make the flower:

* Cut the cardstock into a circle with a 4-inch (10.2 cm) diameter, then cut a spiral into it.

* Pull patterned pink washi from its roll without breaking it. Stick washi to one end of the spiral strip and roll it around the spiral until the entire strip is covered. Cut the washi from its roll (fig. B).

* Wrap the strip into the shape of a flower bud and add glue in between the layers of the strip.

8 To make the leaves:

* Cut a leaf shape out of cardstock.

* Pull green washi from its roll without breaking it. Stick the washi to one end of a cardstock leaf and roll it around and around until the leaf is covered in washi. It's okay for parts of the cardstock to not be covered.

* Repeat to make a second washi leaf.

* Cut a small X near the base of each leaf (fig. C).

9 To make the stem:

* Fold a 3-inch (7.6 cm) piece of yellow washi onto itself lengthwise several times, sticky side to sticky side, so that it becomes a thin strip of washi. Bend and curl one of the ends. Repeat this step to make two more strips.

* Wrap one end of the straw with yellow washi,

A

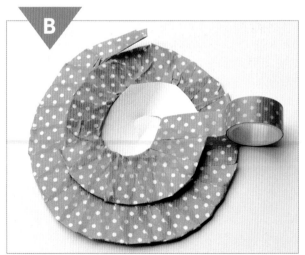

B

placing the three thin strips in between the washi and the straw, with the curled ends extending above the straw.

* Make several fringe cuts on this section of the washi (fig. D).

10 Stick the straw through the center of the flower and position the fringe portion at the flower opening.

Adhere with strong-bonding glue and let it dry. Shape and trim the fringe-cut section of the washi straw (the flower's stamen) as desired. Push the bottom end of the straw through the X shapes on each leaf (fig. E).

11 Place the flower into the bottle vase. Make flowers for the other bottles or fill them with water and fresh flowers. Place all of the bottles into the caddy.

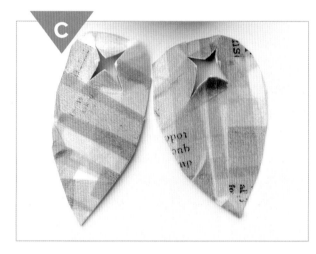

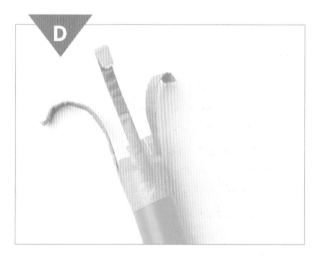

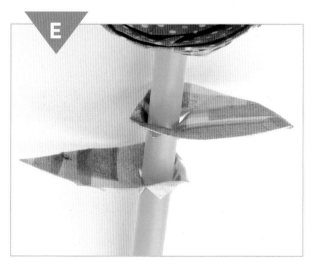

IDEA

Play with the design of the dots to create different patterns. For complex patterns, draw your design on the bottles with a permanent marker before applying the silicone.

chevron nature
DISPLAY JARS

For these cute-as-can-be jars, you make your own washi tape! Applying rubber cement to paper and allowing it to dry creates a repositionable tackiness, much like real washi tape but with your exact preferences for color and style.

DESIGNER: Cynthia Shaffer

WHAT YOU'LL NEED

Basic Washi Kit, page 9
3 upcycled jars with faceted sides, such as jam, mustard, and salad dressing jars
White acrylic paint
Paper plate
Computer with Photoshop or Photoshop Elements
Color printer
White printer paper
Rubber cement

WASHI WONDERFUL

WHAT YOU DO

1 Remove labels from all jars. Thoroughly clean them inside and out, and let them dry.

2 Apply paint to each jar as follows:

* Pour approximately 2 tablespoons of white acrylic paint into one of the jars. Rotate the jar around so the paint covers the entire inside surface of the jar. Add more paint as needed.
* Place the jar upside down on the paper plate and wait 15 minutes. The excess paint will drip onto the paper plate.
* Stand the jar right side up and wait for 15 minutes.
* Repeat until no more excess paint comes out of the jar when you place it upside down. This process may take a total of 4 or 5 hours.

3 Using Photoshop on your computer, create a herringbone pattern as follows:

* Open a new document at U.S. letter size.
* Select and fill the entire document with 50 percent gray, and make your foreground color white.
* Select the brush tool and make the stroke 20 pixels wide and 100 percent hardness. Draw a vertical line every 1 inch (2.5 cm) to make columns. Hint: if you hold the shift button down while drawing, the line will be perfectly straight.
* Draw horizontal lines with ¼-inch (6 mm) spacing until your document is completely gridded.
* Use the rectangular selection tool to select the first column. Next, go to edit/transform/warp and drag each corner on the right side of the selection down 1 inch (2.5 cm), so all the lines in the column are positioned diagonally pointing down to the right. Press enter to confirm this change, and then deselect.

* Select the next column, and follow the same steps as above, except this time drag down the left corners instead. Continue alternating until you have created the herringbone design.
* Set the magic wand tool to "contiguous," and select multiple random gray sections simultaneously by holding down the shift key while selecting with the wand. Fill them with color by going to edit/fill and selecting a color. (I chose gray, purple, pink, yellow, and blue for my colors.)
* Continue until desired colors are complete, then print out your herringbone pattern on white printer paper.

4 Lay the printout on the cutting mat. Cut out a column from the paper using the sharp craft knife and ruler, making sure to center a white vertical line in the middle of your cuts to create the chevron faux washi strips. Cut the strip into equal-length pieces along the diagonal lines, preserving the pointed chevron pattern.

5 Turn the pieces over and apply a layer of rubber cement to the back sides. Let them dry.

6 Stick the faux washi to the bottle facets, alternating chevron orientation between up and down.

7 Fill the jars with found objects from nature, such as sticks and pinecones.

IDEAS

* Make chevron strips shorter, space them further apart vertically, or make multiple rows of chevron bands.
* Paint the found objects to coordinate with your faux washi colors and pattern.

mitered JEWELRY

Have you ever had the perfect outfit but couldn't find matching accessories? Next time you have a fashion crisis, make your own jewelry from washi! Whether you embellish a standing piece or make one from scratch, your new accessories are sure to be the talk of the town.

DESIGNER: Anne Stills

WHAT YOU'LL NEED

Basic Washi Kit, page 9
Washi:
- Dotted pink, standard
- Patterned yellow/pink, thick
- Dotted yellow, standard

5 pieces of thread:
- Three 6-inch (15.2 cm) pieces
- Two 12-inch (30.5 cm) pieces

White beaded necklace
2 ear wires

WHAT YOU DO

Necklace

1 Fold a 6-inch (15.2 cm) piece of thread in half and tie a small loop at the folded end.

2 Cut a 2-inch (5.1 cm) piece of pink dotted washi and lay it on your work surface, sticky side up. Stick the knotted loop onto the washi just below the top edge, then fold the bottom edge of the washi up to cover the loop.

3 Cut an inverted V shape on the lower edge of the washi. Cut the top two corners diagonally to make a V shape. Be careful not to cut the thread.

4 Repeat steps 1 through 3 to make two additional washi dangles.

5 Center and tie one washi dangle on the white beaded necklace. Tie the other two washi dangles onto the necklace, spaced evenly to the left and right from the first dangle.

Earrings

1 Fold a 12-inch (30.5 cm) piece of thread in half and tie a small loop at the folded end.

2 Cut a 2-inch (5.1 cm) piece of yellow/pink patterned washi and lay it on your work surface, sticky side up. Stick the knotted loop to the washi just below the top edge,

then fold the bottom edge of the washi up to cover the loop (fig A).

3 Cut two 1-inch (2.5 cm) pieces of pink dotted washi. Stick one of the pieces onto the thread right above the first washi. Stick the second piece onto the first piece, with the thread sandwiched in between. Repeat with two pieces of yellow dotted washi above the pink washi (fig. B).

4 Cut an inverted V shape on the lower edge of the yellow/pink patterned washi. Cut the top two corners diagonally to make a V shape. Repeat for the pink and yellow washi to complete the first washi earring dangle, being careful not to cut the thread (fig. C).

5 Repeat steps 1 through 4 to create the second washi earring dangle.

6 Tie the washi earring dangles to ear wires, and trim thread ends to desired lengths.

IDEAS

* Use multiple thread strands at once to give the threads a stronger visual presence.
* Cut the washi dangles into different shapes, such as circles, ovals, and squares.

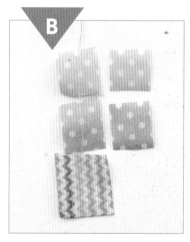

washi fun

WASHI WONDERFUL

stenciled and sprayed
WASHI

DESIGNER: Anne Stills

WHAT YOU'LL NEED

Basic Washi Kit, page 9
White ceramic pitcher
Glass jar
Glass bottle
Liquid acrylic paint,
   cream color
Paper plate
White masking tape
Heavy-duty freezer bag
Stencil objects such as lace
   or a bamboo placemat
Purple spray paint

For a truly creative spin on washi, make your own! Start with masking tape, add stencils and some spray paint, and voilà—one-of-a-kind washi for all your decorating needs.

WHAT YOU DO

1 Remove labels from the bottle and jar. Thoroughly clean the bottle, jar, and pitcher inside and out, and let them dry.

2 To paint the bottle and jar:

* Pour approximately 2 tablespoons of liquid acrylic paint into each. Rotate each container around so that the paint covers the entire inside surface. Add more paint as needed.

* Place the containers upside down on the paper plate and wait 15 minutes. The excess paint will drip onto the paper plate.

* Stand the containers right side up and wait for 15 minutes.

* Repeat until no more excess paint comes out of the containers when you place them upside down. This process may take a total of 4 or 5 hours.

3 To make the stenciled tape:

* Cover one side of the freezer bag with strips of white masking tape (fig. A).
* Lay your chosen stencil objects down on the tape (fig. B).
* Apply a light coat of purple spray paint on top, covering the stencil objects and the tape they are lying on (fig. C).
* Let the paint dry completely and remove the stencil objects (fig. D).

4 Peel the tape off of the bag and stick the strips onto the pitcher and the painted bottle and jar.

IDEAS

* Experiment with different types of stencils.
* Try elevating the stencil off the masking tape while you're applying the spray paint to get a softer stencil effect.
* Try layering stencil patterns with different colors to make extremely unique "washi" designs.

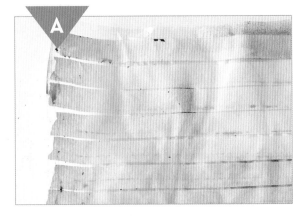

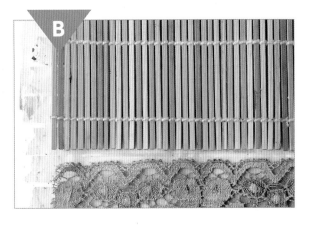

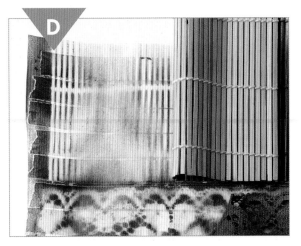

candy-coordinated JARS

Designer: Anne Stills

Creative Idea: Fold a 12-inch (30.5 cm) strip of washi in half, sticky sides facing each other, to make a 6-inch (15.2 cm) piece. Use a pencil to mark the center point then mark halfway between the center and both ends. At the first mark, cut halfway through the width of the washi from the top to bottom. Repeat at the center mark. At the third mark, cut halfway through the width of the tape in the opposite direction, from bottom to top. Bend the washi in an S-curve until all three cuts match up, and interlock them together. The bow will now hold its shape. Trim the ends and cut a V shape at both ends.

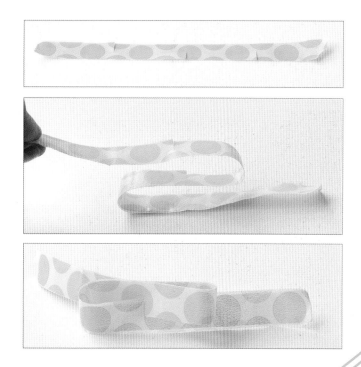

WASHI WONDERFUL

spiced-up
SERVING UTENSILS

DESIGNER: Carolyn Garris

WHAT YOU'LL NEED

Basic Washi Kit, page 9
Washi:
- Striped black/white, standard
- Dotted black/white, thin
- Patterned black/white, standard
- Patterned blue/white, standard
- Patterned green/white, standard
- Patterned blue/orange, standard
- Striped blue/orange, standard

Wooden serving utensils: three spoons,
two forks, two paddles*
Painter's tape
Plastic bags
Acrylic paint: white, orange, and light blue
Small paintbrush
Container with water (for rinsing)
Clear gloss spray sealer**

* Wooden serving utensils are available at
grocery stores and kitchen supply stores.
They come in assorted thicknesses and
heights, all of which can be embellished
with washi using these methods.

** Spraying the decorated handles with
spray sealer will make the utensils water-
resistant but not waterproof. Gentle hand
washing is recommended, but do not
submerge in water or put them in
the dishwasher.

*Bored with your plain serving
utensils? Dress them up with washi!
With a little spray sealer, you can
spruce up utensils to match any
mood or event.*

WHAT YOU DO

Three Spoons

1 Cover the upper neck of a spoon's handle with painter's
tape. Place the spoon end and upper neck into a plastic bag
and tape it shut with painter's tape, allowing the tape to
slightly overlap the tape on the handle for a secure seal.

2 Apply two to three coats of white acrylic paint to the
exposed part of the wooden spoon with a small paintbrush,
allowing each coat to dry.

3 Repeat steps 1 and 2 with the other two serving spoons.

4 Carefully remove the painter's tape and plastic bags from
the spoons and set it all aside to use again in step 7.

5 On one spoon, wrap two pieces of striped black/white
washi around the top, middle, and bottom of the painted
handle, leaving space between each set of washi strips
(fig. A on the next page).

6 On the other two spoons, wrap patterned black/white washi and dotted black/white washi, allowing some of the painted areas to show through.

7 Wrap up the spoons again with the painter's tape and plastic bags from step 4. Spray the handles of all the wooden spoons with clear gloss spray sealer. Let dry. Remove the painter's tape and plastic bags.

Fork and Paddle #1

1 Repeat steps 1 through 4 of Three Spoons for both the fork and paddle.

2 Wrap a strip of patterned blue/white washi in a diagonal around the fork, allowing a small strip of the painted areas to show through. Repeat with a strip of patterned green/white washi to cover the paddle (fig. B).

3 Wrap up utensils again with the painter's tape and plastic bags. Spray the handles with clear gloss spray sealer. Let dry. Remove the painter's tape and plastic bags.

Fork and Paddle #2

1 Repeat step 1 of Three Spoons for both the fork and paddle.

2 Cover the lower part of the fork's handle with painter's tape, leaving 1 inch (2.5 cm) exposed at the bottom. Paint the lowest section with orange acrylic paint. Let dry.

3 Cover the orange painted area with painter's tape, then measure 1 inch (2.5 cm) above it and wrap another length of painter's tape around the handle. Paint the exposed section with light blue acrylic paint. Let dry.

4 Repeat step 3 three more times, alternating 1-inch (2.5 cm) bands of orange and blue paint up the handle.

5 Wrap five small pieces of patterned blue/orange washi around the handle at the points where the orange and light blue paints meet. This will help cover up any irregularities in the paint job (fig. C).

6 Repeat steps 1 through 5 with the wooden paddle, starting with the light blue paint at the lowest exposed 1 inch (2.5 cm) of the utensil.

7 Wrap up the utensils again with the painter's tape and plastic bags. Spray the handles with clear gloss spray sealer. Let dry. Remove the painter's tape and plastic bags.

A

B

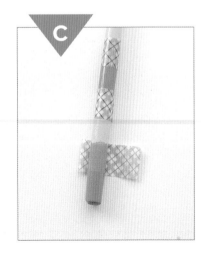

C

WASHI WONDERFUL

decorated CANS

Designer: Carolyn Garris

Creative Idea: After you clean and dry upcycled cans, spray paint them inside and out and let them dry. Stick multiple pieces of washi in coordinating colors onto the exterior of the cans. On some cans, stick strips of washi to the inner top edge.

animal toy-topped HOLIDAY JARS

Designer: Anne Stills

Creative Idea: For the jar tops, spray paint the lids and plastic animal figures. Glue the figures onto the lids with a strong-hold glue. To make a fringed decoration:

* Fold a 4-inch (10.2 cm) strip of washi in half, sticky sides facing, to make a 2-inch (5.1 cm) strip. Stick the strip horizontally on a piece of vellum with washi that narrowly overlaps the top edge.

* Fold another piece of washi the same length and adhere it to the vellum above and slightly overlapping the first piece.

* Repeat to make a vertical row of washi strips approximately 4 inches (10.2 cm) high.

* Turn over the vellum and draw the desired shape (tree, pumpkin, egg) on the back. Cut it out.

* Peel off the bottom layer, make fringed cuts along the bottom edge, and stick it to the front of the jar. Repeat on up the row of washi strips until entire shape has been transferred.

A

light switch COVERS

A plain white light switch plate is a blank canvas just waiting to be embellished. Choose washi to match the room, and since it's so easy to remove, you can change it down the road if you'd like.

DESIGNER: Carolyn Garris

WHAT YOU'LL NEED

Basic Washi Kit, page 9
Washi:
- Patterned blue/orange, standard
- Striped orange, standard
- Patterned blue, standard
- Striped blue/white, standard
- Zigzag blue/orange, standard
- Dotted orange, standard
- Assorted colors and patterns as desired

Light switch plates, 3¼ x 5 inches (8.3 x 12.7 cm)

WHAT YOU DO

1 Remove the screws from the light switch plate and set them aside.

2 Place the light switch plate on your work surface vertically. Stick a 2½-inch (6.4 cm) piece of patterned blue/orange washi horizontally at the center left portion of the plate, bending the ends of the tape to the back at the left and down through the rectangular hole. Repeat this process with a second piece of the same washi on the center right portion of the plate.

3 Center and stick a 4½-inch (11.4 cm) piece of striped orange washi right beneath the washi from step 2 so that they are abutting right against one another. Use the sharp craft knife to cut away a small section at the center top edge so it doesn't obstruct the rectangular hole.

4 Center and stick three additional pieces of washi in various colors and patterns to cover the lower part of the plate. For the bottom strip, curve the bottom edge of the washi and then fold down the two short sides, for a slight mitered effect.

5 Rotate the plate 180 degrees and repeat steps 3 and 4 (fig. A).

6 Repeat steps 1 through 5 with different colors and patterns of washi to create different styles of light switch plates.

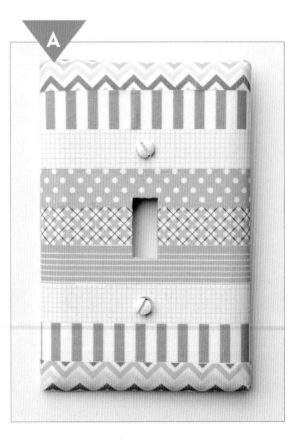

A

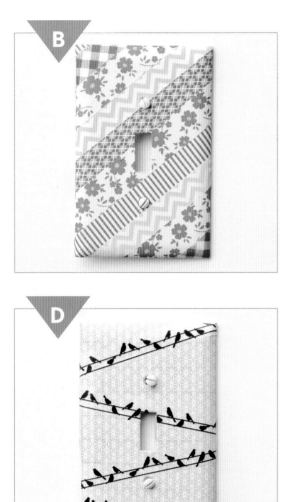

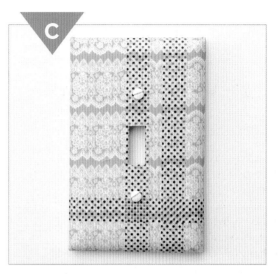

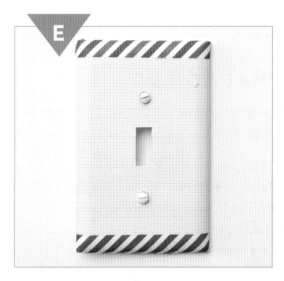

VARIATIONS

* For a slightly different effect, follow steps 1 through 5 to cover a plate but slant the washi diagonally (fig. B).
* Cover an entire switch plate with a patterned color. On top of that, stick two vertical strips and one horizontal strip of a contrasting color. Use a sharp craft knife to cut away any washi that obstructs the center rectangular hole (fig. C).

* Cover an entire switch plate with a patterned color. Then add four strips of washi diagonally in a zigzag pattern. Use the sharp craft knife to cut away any washi that obstructs the center rectangular hole (fig. D).
* Cover an entire switch plate with checked blue/white washi then stick a strip of air-mail patterned washi at the top and bottom edges. This will create an envelope effect (fig. E).

washi fun

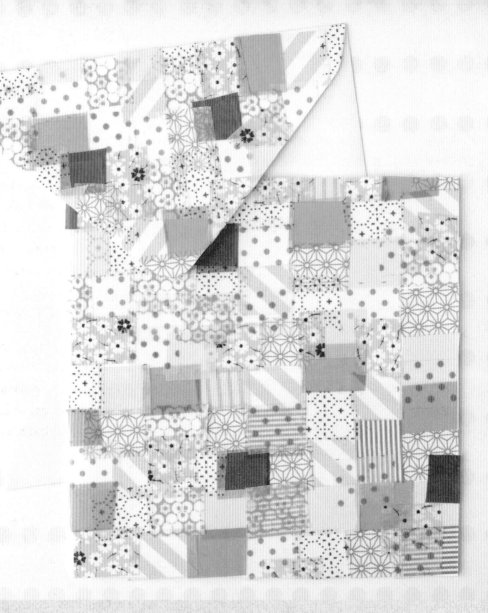

patchwork STATIONERY

For the ultimate in vibrant, handmade stationery, create a patchwork of washi on cards and envelopes. Select your color palette according to the season or occasion for a truly personal touch.

DESIGNER: Ishtar Olivera Belart

WHAT YOU'LL NEED

Basic Washi Kit, page 9
Washi: assorted patterns and
  colors, standard
Blank, pre-folded card and
  matching envelope (in
  whatever size you like)

WHAT YOU DO

1 Cut a wide variety of washi (both patterned and solid styles) into small squares. The squares do not have to be precisely the same size, but should range somewhere between ¾ inch (1.9 cm) and 1 inch (2.5 cm) in length. As you cut the squares, attach them to the edge of a table randomly. The number of squares you'll need depends on the size of your card and envelope.

2 Starting in the lower left-hand corner, attach the washi squares to the front of the card. In order to achieve a random patchwork style, do not look at which piece you are picking up next and allow a random order of colors and patterns to happen. Cover the entire front of the card with washi squares.

3 Attach washi squares to the flap of the matching envelope in a smilar manner. Trim the excess washi on the flap's edges with scissors.

139

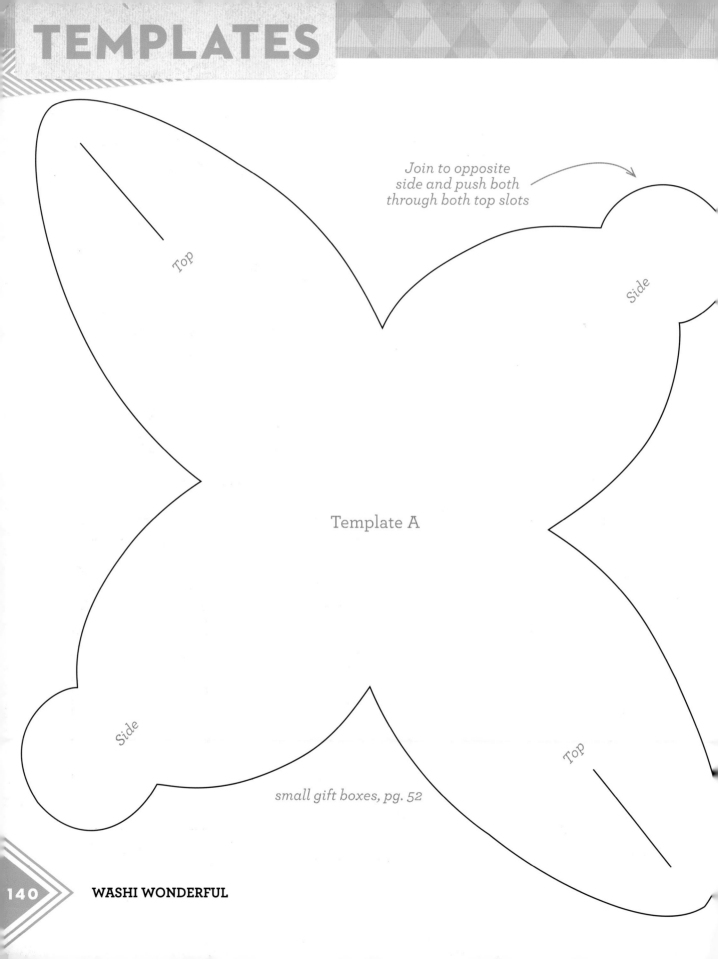

Join to opposite side and push both through both top slots

Top

Side

Template A

Side

small gift boxes, pg. 52

Top

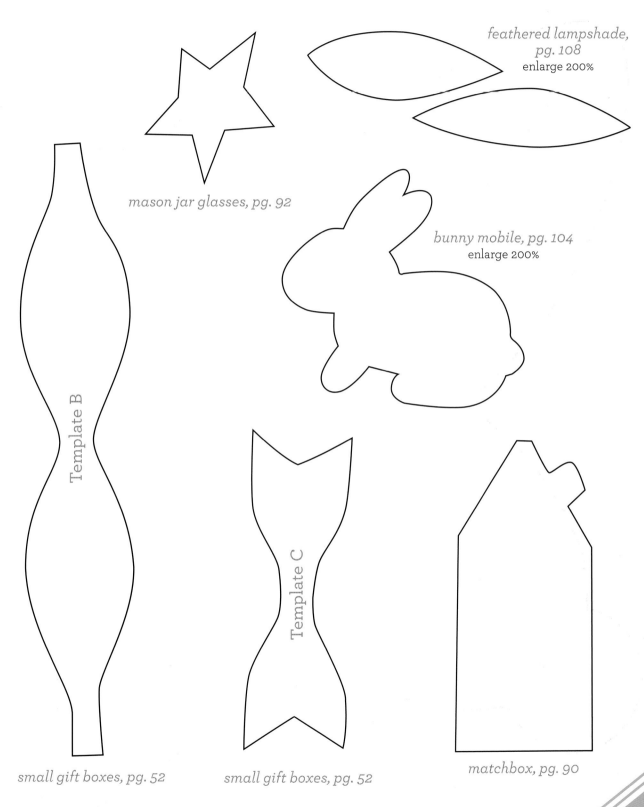

*feathered lampshade,
pg. 108*
enlarge 200%

mason jar glasses, pg. 92

bunny mobile, pg. 104
enlarge 200%

Template B

Template C

small gift boxes, pg. 52

small gift boxes, pg. 52

matchbox, pg. 90

about the
CONTRIBUTORS

Ishtar Olivera Belart is an illustrator from Spain, whose love for art began at an early age. She has illustrated children's books and designed rubber stamps for Penny Black, and she also teaches craft workshops. She lives in England, where she enjoys taking walks through the forest with her two sons, Tuti and Keni. Visit *www.ishtarolivera.com.*

Carolyn Garris is a marketing consultant and blogger who lives in Los Angeles with her husband, son, and dog. Carolyn enjoys providing creative and inspirational tutorials on her blog, be it a crafting project, a recipe, home décor, or lifestyle. Visit *www.carolynshomework.blogspot.com.*

Avital Gertner-Samet lives in the Bay Area in California and searches the boundaries of her creativity. Through her blog and her book, *Unleashing the Creative Child Within You,* Avital takes her readers along with her on her creative journey. Avital is also an attorney, wife, and mother. Visit *www.creativityprompt.com.*

Cynthia Shaffer is a mixed-media artist, quilter, and creative sewer. She is author of *Stash Happy Patchwork* (Lark, 2011) and *Stash Happy Appliqué* (Lark, 2012). Cynthia lives in Orange, California, with her husband, Scott; her sons, Corry and Cameron; and her beloved Boston Terriers. Visit *www.cynthiashaffer.com.*

Anne Stills loves the creative process—especially related to her passion for jewelry art, mixed-media art, and photography. She lives in southern California and enjoys spending time outdoors with her family. Visit *www.sunsetstills.com.*

WASHI TAPE

Depending on where you live, you may not find washi tape in your local stores. Some crafts stores don't carry it at all or only stock a limited selection. If you get a blank look when you ask for washi, try asking for decorative tape. Your best bet is to check the scrapbooking section.

Online is a different story! There are hundreds of options made by different manufacturers in a wide range of prices, in rolls and sometimes in sheets. Again, it's not always called washi. When comparing, check the length of the tape so you know how much is on the roll. And any smart shopper knows that different websites often sell the same product at different prices. Shop around, and look for free shipping and other promotions.

www.acherryontop.com
www.amazon.com
www.artisticartifacts.com
www.consumercrafts.com
www.cutetape.com
www.downtowntape.com
www.etsy.com/shop/prettytape
www.ginkopapers.com
www.happytape.bigcartel.com
www.hsn.com
www.joann.com

www.koyalwholesale.com
www.paper-source.com
www.scrapbook.com
www.simonsaysstamp.com
www.tapeswell.com
www.thepaperparlour.co.uk
www.twopeasinabucket.com
www.wishywashi.com

OTHER SUPPLIES

Some of the suppliers listed for washi tape also carry scrapbooking and other supplies you may need for projects in this book, such as paper punches, adhesives, glitter, rubber stamps, and so forth. Most supplies can be found in craft stores, department stores, or office supply stores. Here are some additional online sources.

Art Supplies

Look here for special papers (including transparent vellum, kraft paper, butcher paper, and blank cards), alphabet stamps, inkpads, acrylic paint, paintbrushes, and so forth.

www.artsupply.com
www.artsupplywarehouse.com

www.cheapjoes.com
www.dharmatrading.com
www.dickblick.com
www.jacquardproducts.com
www.jerrysartarama.com
www.lcipaper.com
www.michaels.com
www.misterart.com
www.origamipaperstore.com
www.paper-source.com
www.papermart.com
www.simplystamps.com
www.stampinup.com
www.utrechtart.com

Craft Supplies

Most of these suppliers carry paper punches, baker's twine, and scrapbooking supplies in general.

shop.hobbylobby.com
shop.marthastewart.com
www.acmoore.com
www.eksuccessbrands.com
www.herrschners.com
www.mcgillinc.com
www.ohmycrafts.com
www.save-on-crafts.com
www.staples.com
www.target.com
www.uchida.com

INDEX

Editor: **LINDA KOPP**
Art Director: **KRISTI PFEFFER**
Graphic Designer: **RAQUEL JOYA**
Writer: **AMANDA CRABTREE WESTON**
Copyeditor: **NANCY D. WOOD**
Assistant Editors: **KERRI WINTERSTEIN,
MONICA MOUET, ANTONIA SILVA**

about the author

Jenny Doh is head of *www.crescendoh. com*. She has authored and packaged numerous books including *Craft-a-Doodle, Crochet Love, Print Collective, Creative Lettering, Stamp It!, Journal It!, We Make Dolls!,* and *Hand in Hand.* She lives in Santa Ana, California, and loves to create, stay fit, and play music.